The publisher of this book is generously donating all royalties from the retail sales of **"REMARKABLE RETIREMENT 02"** to:

LEMONADE DAY

America was built on the back of small business. Entrepreneurs take risks believing they can realize their dream if they work hard, take responsibility and act as good stewards of their resources. Today's youth share that optimism but lack the life skills, mentorship and real-world experience necessary to be successful. In 2007, founder Michael Holthouse had a vision to empower today's youth to become tomorrow's entrepreneurs through helping them start, own and operate their very own business… a lemonade stand.

Lemonade Day is a strategic 14-step process that walks youth from a dream to a business plan while teaching them the same principles required to start any big company. Inspiring kids to work hard and make a profit, they are also taught to spend some, save some and share some by giving back to their community.

Since its launch in 2007 in Houston Texas, Lemonade Day has grown from serving 2,700 kids in one city to 1 million children across North America. With the help of partners like Google for Entrepreneurs, Lemonade Day will continue to spark the spirit of entrepreneurship and empower youth to set goals, work hard, and achieve their dreams.

You can learn more about Lemonade Day by visiting:
www.LemonadeDay.org

REMARKABLE RETIREMENT

Conversations with Leading Retirement Experts and Financial Advisors

VOLUME 2

By Remarkable Press™

DISCLAIMER AND/OR LEGAL NOTICES:

The information presented in this book represents the views of the author as of the date of publication. The author reserves the rights to alter and update their opinions based on new conditions. This book is for informational purposes only.

Remarkable Retirement Volume 2/ Mark Imperial. —1st ed.

Managing Editor/ Stewart Andrew Alexander

ISBN-13: 978-0-9987085-7-7

CONTENTS

A NOTE TO THE READER

Thank you for buying your copy of "Remarkable Retirement Volume 2: Conversations with Leading Retirement Experts and Financial Advisors." This book was originally created as a series of live interviews, that's why it reads like a series of conversations, rather than a traditional book that talks at you.

I wanted you to feel as though the participants and I are talking with you, much like a close friend, or relative, and felt that creating the material this way would make it easier for you to grasp the topics and put them to use quickly, rather than wading through hundreds of pages.

So grab a pen, take notes and get ready to learn some fascinating insights and real-world experiences.

Warmest regards,

Mark Imperial
Author and Radio Personality

INTRODUCTION

"Remarkable Retirement Volume 2: Conversations with Leading Retirement Experts and Financial Advisors" is a collaborative book series featuring leading Professionals from across the country who are passionate about helping individuals considering their retirement option

Remarkable Press™ would like to extend a heartfelt thank you to all participants who took the time to submit their chapter and offer their support in becoming 'Get the word out Ambassadors' for this project.

Remarkable Press™ has pledged 100% of the royalties from the retail sales of this book to be donated to Lemonade Day. Should you want to make a direct donation, visit their website at: www.LemonadeDay.org

LEON C. LABRECQUE
JD, CPA, CFP®, CFA

Managing Partner and CEO
LJPR Financial Advisors

Email: leon.labrecque@ljpr.com
Website: https://www.ljpr.com
LinkedIn: https://linkedin.com/in/leonlabrecque
Facebook: www.facebook.com/ljprfa
Twitter: https://twitter.com/leonlabrecque
Call: (248) 641-7400

"The more you know, the more time you can spend enjoying life, rather than worrying."

For Leon LaBrecque, who has been featured in media outlets like InvestmentNews, CNBC, USA Today and Forbes, reducing uncertainty is a theme that runs throughout his professional life.

As a practicing attorney, CPA, CFP®, and CFA, he is an educator at heart and has a passion for helping others fully understand their financial lives.

In pursuit of elevating financial literacy through the use of brains, passion, and courage, LaBrecque launched LJPR Pride, the financial education arm of his firm that serves students and all demographics.

He has authored several books and proprietary financial programs for General Motors, Ford Motor Company, AT&T and numerous law enforcement organizations.

When he's not helping people prepare for a thriving retirement, he enjoys spending time with his family, hunting, and fishing in Michigan's beautiful outdoors, and relaxing through yoga and poetry.

MIND OVER MONEY: THE BUSY WOMAN'S NOTION OF BANDWIDTH
By Leon C. LaBrecque

Describe the clients you work with and the types of situations they find themselves in when they come to you for your help?

I help busy female professionals to understand and implement strategies to improve their family's wellbeing, so they can increase their bandwidth: "money, time, happiness and love."

Why busy female professionals?

First, I find that a lot of women get in a crush between managing a career, a family, and sometimes adult parents. I also find that the levels of complexity in all of those areas are daunting. Trying to figure out 401(k) investments, their estate plan, their mom's estate plan, and the kid's college funding is a movie with a lot of moving parts. To help, we've built a team where someone can get a one-stop shop. One stop in that someone can get their questions answered without going to six different places and getting six different answers.

What's bandwidth? I did a TEDx talk on this. We, as humans have a finite amount of 'room' or space to process our lives. Think about four things:

- Money
- Time
- Happiness
- Love.

Think of those things occupying a pipeline. The pipe has a defined width, so it can only accommodate a limited amount of the flow of those items. We only have a limited amount of time (86,400 seconds a day), a limited amount of money, and those can limit our happiness and then, our ability to love and be loved. But we can increase our bandwidth. If our band was a physical pipe, it would provide 9 times the volume for every increase of one unit in the radius. Adding more time, through maybe auto-bill pay, or having a bullet journal, increase the bandwidth. Having our 401(k) auto-rebalance saves time and reduces risk, increasing happiness.

So the idea here is to take some things off your plate. We want you to look at the big picture, and determine your strategy; to work on what's important and not what's mundane, to take some of the research and even the actions off your plate, so you can do what you need to do and what you want to do. So you can have more bandwidth.

What common obstacles prevent your clients from managing the big picture?

I find that busy professional women tend to get in a time crunch over how many possibilities there are in a financial decision. Consider that in 2016, there were 9,511 mutual funds in the United States. If we consider the simple aspect of mutual funds selection, that decision in itself is crushing in the time involved. Now add stocks, ETFs, IRA decisions, 529 plan decisions, estate planning questions, and we can sink into 'analysis paralysis.' So a big problem is how much we need to analyze to get a good decision. How much business TV? How many websites? How many blogs? Newsletters? Books? Someone needs to separate the forest from the trees.

Another problem is prioritizing goals. Suppose Susan has a 90-year old mom she is helping, a 28-year-old daughter she is helping, a household to maintain, and a career and business decisions to juggle. Sometimes you hear the phrase 'sandwich caregiver,' but it's more like a club sandwich: more layers squeezing. She gets into one rabbit hole and the other suffers. She needs to see the big picture and either auto-pilot or delegate tasks, so she can focus on the thing she does best.

Action is another problem. We know we should do something (like eat healthily or exercise more), but we don't pull the trigger. For whatever reason, fear, time, or complacency; we tend to avoid the actual action. So I may tell you to rebalance your portfolio, or check your beneficiaries, or get your estate plan done, but it doesn't happen until you do it. Someone said I think Amelia Earhart, "The best way to do it is to do it."

Time crunch from information overload, getting too many goals in front of us and failing actually to act on the plan, are the main obstacles I see to effectively increasing bandwidth and doing what you want to do.

How would you help busy female professionals to manage the big picture, and what kind of results do you typically see?

A typical case was my friend and client Jessica (I changed her name). She had a Ph.D. in chemistry and worked for a big drug company. I met her at a seminar I was doing for the company on retirement planning. Jessica came up after the session, and we arranged a meeting. She's brilliant, so I expected everything to be in order. Some things were, and some weren't.

She was a great saver: she had saved a bunch of money but was scared that she didn't have enough. She didn't have an estate plan, wanted to expand her lake house, but wasn't sure she should or could. Her investments were all in the same funds she had used most of her career, and she had almost 25% of her 401(k) in her company stock, as well as stock outside of her plan.

She was the classic case of analysis/paralysis. Here was this brilliant scientist who forgot more about math than I knew (and actually, I'm quite good at math), unable to make a simple decision like whether she could retire (she could); figure out if she could afford to expand her lake house (she could); or balance her 401(k) plan (she needed to). She also needed to pull the trigger on a lot of things.

I think sometimes I work a lot more on behavior than on investments or taxes or estates. So the first order of business was to show a very smart person that she could afford to do what she wanted to do. Luckily, it's not hard to show a Ph.D. that a 3% return on her investments was more than enough to live on, and was actually more than she was making on an after-tax/after-saving basis when she was working at the company.

What was a little tougher was to get her to make a move, but with some patience, we got the plan going. Next order of business? To fix up the lake house. This was a bit easier since her heirs consisted of distant nieces and nephews. The simple question of what they would do with the lake house got that project moving, with the help of a well-funded bank account. We made a donation to her college with some appreciated company stock. She loves her life now, and travels between two houses and has bridge parties and friends enjoying her lake house.

It's about getting organized. It's about getting started.

What common misconceptions prevent the busy female professionals you work with from achieving their retirement goals?

People have a lot of misconceptions about markets, retirement, and planning. One common misconception is the 'zero-sum game' myth. This is the myth that 'somebody wins/somebody loses,' or the notion that in every transaction the win and loss are equal.

When I hear this one, I usually ask the person to take out their smartphone. I point out that the smartphone replaces a bunch of things, like a map, a camera, a phone, a library, a copy machine, a digital assistant, a calendar; yet those all still exist. I suggest the world is expansive, and we all want our lives to be better.

Another myth is the 'time the market' myth. Here, I usually see one of two questions: 'Will you get out before the market goes down?' or 'Will you get out if the market goes down?'

I answer the first one with the observation that if I could determine the prior direction of the market, I would not be talking to anyone, and instead, I'd be enjoying the big island of Hawaii, which would be renamed 'Leon.'

On the second question, I answer quite simply that down markets are sales, and that all prior market declines were followed by recoveries.

Then there's the myth of 'I can't afford to retire.' Here, people usually fail to look at the bottom line of the retirement decision.

Here's what I mean:

Suppose Sarah works at a decent job, making about $9,000 per month. She nets, after federal, state, Social Security and Medicare taxes, her 401(k) contribution and her job-related expenses about $5,100 a month. She can get a pension from her employer of $4,050 a month. She starts thinking that $9,000 is way more than $4,050 and she can't afford to retire.

However, her pension check is not subject to 401(k), Social Security, Medicare or Job-related expenses. In addition, she'll be in a lower income tax bracket. She will likely net around

$3,600. There is a big difference between the gross comparison ($4,950) and the net comparison ($1,500). If she has a 401(k) balance of $600,000, she can take a 3% withdrawal and make up most of it. And... we haven't gotten to Social security yet. Bottom line is: it's the bottom line.

Probably one of the biggest misconceptions is how people in this business get paid and who they work for. There are literally hundreds of thousands of people in the financial services business. Most get paid a commission and work for a company. So they sell insurance or commission-based products. More importantly, they work for the company they represent, which means they act in the best interest of their company.

As to their customer, they need only determine if the investment they are selling is 'suitable' for the client. This is vastly different from a fee-only advisor, who acts as a fiduciary to the client. Here the advisor acts in the interest of the client and works for the client.

What mistakes should the busy female professionals be aware of?

A big mistake I see busy women make is not getting enough good information to make a decision. We had a client whose mother was in need of extended care. She immediately did a quick google search of what to do and concluded she needed to sell all of her mom's assets including the house and give the money to her and her brothers.

What she didn't look into was the complicated 'look-back' rules of Medicaid, and worse, she didn't think it was important that her Dad has been a veteran and was eligible for VA benefits. Many months and dollars later, with the help of an elder care expert, we sorted most of it out. Jumping the gun can be very painful in planning.

Another pitfall is being inundated with information and advice, without being able to assimilate the data and make a good plan. Without a plan, we tend to act on emotion, which usually doesn't work out.

A good case in point is what I call the 'fear/greed' dichotomy. When the market is low, I typically get the question "why do we have stocks? aren't they risky?" I then explain we want stocks to perform for us and they are balanced by bonds which tend to protect the portfolio. Conversely, when the market is high, I hear "why do we have bonds? why not more stocks?"

Many people get afraid when the stock market is down and greedy when it is up. In actuality, you should be doing the opposite of that: buy more stock when the stock market is low and more bonds when the stock market is high.

So we have too little information and too much information, and then we have just plain old bad information. This is the advice from the gym, or from friends, or the clever brother-in-law. This might be annuities for safety (safe with poor return and huge fees), or timing (which no major pension plan or individual investor uses as a main investment strategy or goofy things like bitcoin, or gold, or Iraqi dinar (yes, that was a rage).

When faced with the question of a bad idea, I usually pose, 'How many <x add in whatever it is> do you think Bill Gates has?' If that doesn't work, I then resort to logic, reasoning and some good charts. If that doesn't work, I politely suggest that I can't be a part of this great idea since I disagree with it and offer to spin off an amount that they can use to purchase the 'great' idea. Most of the time, plan A works.

What we don't know, what we feel, and what we think we know can be obstructions to our successful planning. We have to set aside our biases and pay attention to information before we act.

What common fears prevent busy female professionals from having the money, time, happiness and love they desire?

Sometimes we will see folks after knowing them for many years. Usually, they comment that they wish they had started earlier. I ask why, and the response usually includes 'I thought I wasn't big enough to get this kind of advice,' or 'I (or my mom or someone I know) got burned, and I don't trust the business.'

That first fear is common, where people feel they don't have enough to matter to a professional advisor. Well, this is nonsense from a good advisor's standpoint. I view my mission to take care of people's money, and it doesn't matter what level that is. Clearly, advisors spend more time on more complex situations and the larger the amount of money to plan with; the more work is involved.

People should know that all good advisors are there to help, even if it means referring to another advisor. You may not need the Mayo Clinic, but you might clearly need a doctor. Get assistance.

The second reason, which I call the 'Madoff reason,' is a legitimate fear. When the Madoff scandal came out, my mom (who is now 97), called me and asked if we had any money with Madoff. I told her no. She said, 'I can't believe there are crooks like that.' I said, 'I can't believe you've been around this long and didn't believe there are crooks.'

You need to check backgrounds, do broker checks, and most importantly, use the smell test about what someone promises you. Madoff was reporting significant positive returns every single month, yet almost no one questioned it.

Why would the busy female professionals you help want to improve their families wellbeing?

We are all faced with limited bandwidth. We only have so much time and so much money, which leads to prospectively so much happiness and consequently, love. Busy women want more of all of those things. Some are interrelated, like using auto-bill pay saves time and money.

Automating savings into a 401(k) or other plan saves time and provides happiness while reducing stress. Setting aside money for a child or grandchild's education gives satisfaction and well-being.

Our busy lives are filled with activities that compete for our time, money, happiness and love. Focusing on what is important can be life-changing. And by far, money is the least limited of our bandwidth. Heck, we can make more money. Get a gig job, freelance, work overtime. Time is a different story.

We're given 86,400 seconds every day when they are gone; they are gone. Time is a precious resource. And happiness usually comes from solving problems.

If we help another solve their problem, it makes us feel good. And finally, sharing joy and love is what makes this whole seven-layer carrot cake of life worth living. But bandwidth involves the interface of those things.

We save time and money to allow us to solve problems to be happy, so we can love more.

Sure, I can talk about retirement security, or markets, or taxes, or law, but the bottom line is your life and your satisfaction with it.

What led you to where you are and what you do today?

A lot of people ask me how I chose this path. I had a music scholarship and a couple of academic scholarships. I thought I wanted to be an engineer.

Then in a scholarship interview, I told the committee that I wanted to be a lawyer. They suggested that I needed an undergraduate degree, so I asked what was hard and required math. They said accounting. I asked how that worked. The response was 'No one understands all of the tax law.'

To me, that was the challenge. How can I take something complex and make it useful? How can I help people get what they want? How do I do this as a servant and not a salesman?

My parents both went through the Depression. I grew up in a lower middle class, blue-collar suburb of Detroit and worked from the day I turned 14. I watched what hard work could do, but I also saw what understanding how things worked could do.

From my earliest years, I always wanted to 'figure it out' and solve the problem. The area I'm in is perfect: it's complicated, it's ever-changing, and it has millions of people needing help with it. Just my style.

What are your final thoughts for busy female professionals who want to improve their family's wellbeing, so they can increase their bandwidth?

So I have some final thoughts for the busy woman professional who wants to achieve a sense of financial well-being and increase her bandwidth. Like any good goal set it in writing.

Make it specific (what do you want, when?), measurable (how much and how do we succeed?), achievable (we can't do it if we can't do it), realistic (hard to retire on $100,000 a year if you make $50,000) and timely (when do you get done?) Yes, I borrowed the SMART goals, but they work.

The other ingredient is getting help. If I want to get healthy, I may need a doctor. I likely need a dentist, I might want a trainer. If I want to build a house, I might be able to do it all myself, but I likely want a plumber and an electrician at the minimum.

In other words, consider getting some help.

I'm pretty smart, but I call a plumber to do my plumbing. The cost is worth it, and the mess is too ugly if I goof up. I think money is a lot like that: the mess can be ugly if you fail.

If the reader wants to know more, how can they connect with you?

I have a nice tool that readers will find useful. Over the years, I've compiled a checklist of simple financial, estate and retirement planning tips that are mostly common sense, like 'take a selfie of the contents of your house.'

These are assembled in a PDF document called, 'Small Good Choices™' which is available at http://ljpr.com/wp-content/uploads/2017/08/Small-Good-Choices-Booklet.pdf.

A whole series of our other books are available on our website www.ljpr.com under 'Financial Literacy.'

To ask a question, please contact me at info@ljpr.com.

WILLIAM N. KEARNEY
SERIES 65 FIDUCIARY

Bill Kearney, Founder & President
Integrated Financial Concepts, LLC

Email: AskUs@ifcadvisors.com
Website: http://www.ifcadvisors.com
LinkedIn: https://linkedin.com/in/billkearneyifc
Facebook: Integrated Financial Concepts, LLC
Twitter: https://twitter.com/retire_stronger
Call: (704) 895-3003 / **Call:** (704) 728-6832

Bill became a financial planner because he is passionate about people and finances. He believes that most people are inherently wise and understand that they need a financial roadmap to follow. But their problem is that they just can't find an adviser in whom they trust, so they go without a plan. And unfortunately, they soon find out that traveling the retirement journey without a well-designed roadmap is not a good idea.

Money is important, but really, money is just fuel for your journey through life. Holistic planning ensures that money is put to its highest and best use, which, in large part, will determine how enjoyable your journey will be.

Bill graduated from the University of Tennessee in 2001 and again in 2003. Shortly after graduating, he started his career in financial services. He learned pretty quickly that being independent would allow him to be unbiased and holistic in his planning practice. When you work for a company, there is always the corporate push to sell their products.

Bill's focus is to choose the very best for his clients and being an independent Fiduciary gives him the ability to shop the market and make superior recommendations without external pressure to sell or produce.

RETIREMENT INCOME PLANNING
MYTHS & MISCONCEPTIONS
By Bill Kearney

How does Bill Kearney and Integrated Financial Concepts, LLC help consumers?

I help people create retirement income plans so that they can enjoy their golden years doing what they desire and not having to stress over money or finances. I meet most of my clients through the adult financial literacy courses I teach at a local community college, so by the time I get to sit down with them one-on-one, they know better than ever that they need a plan and the dangers of not having one.

Many of the people who come to see me can be described like this: They realize now that they are on a journey that will end somewhere, they may or may not have attempted to plan for this journey previously, and now know that while they have a desired destination in mind, their success in reaching the destination is unclear.

Look, everyone is trying to get from here to there. "Here" is where you are right now. "There" is peace of mind. Isn't that true? At the end of the day, aren't you working, saving, growing and preserving your income so that you can put your head on the pillow in retirement and have peace of mind?

From here, everything looks terrific. But sadly, most people don't end up achieving peace of mind. They don't fulfill their goals, or their money doesn't grow as planned. They retire and can draw less income than anticipated, or they have healthcare issues they never thought would happen to them. So now, getting from here to there isn't so easy. Yet strangely enough, most people still just kind of wing it. So imagine if you stepped out onto the street in New York, with an ultimate destination of California without a map or a GPS. You might get there, but it may be a really difficult journey, or you might not get there at all.

What common obstacles prevent your clients from creating a retirement income plan?

I would say the biggest obstacle to creating a plan is a lack of trust in people in my field. Can you blame the folks for not trusting us? We've all seen the headlines of investors being swindled for hundreds of thousands and in some cases millions of dollars. No one wants to end up in that situation and how will you know if it's happening to you before it's too late? So as I said earlier, most people just wing it.

They use a different person for insurance, accounting, estate planning, and investment management and sadly, these people never talk to one another. If they do communicate, often times they are providing conflicting information about other parts of your financial picture.

I believe that most people are inherently wise and understand that they need a plan, a roadmap to follow. But their problem is that they just can't find an advisor in whom they trust enough to get one, so they go without. And unfortunately, they soon find out that traveling the retirement journey without a well-designed roadmap can become difficult.

And let's not overlook the fact that there are about 100 other things you could be doing besides financial planning that is definitely more enjoyable, so it's really easy to put it off. I know this is true and I'm really not offended by it in any way. Some of this thinking, however, comes from the lack of trust and the difficulty to change concepts previously mentioned. If you don't have trust, and you find change difficult, you're likely to find *anything else* more enjoyable than building a retirement income plan.

Another big issue is lack of emotion. I can do a lot of things as a planner to help you see what your financial picture looks like currently as well as what it may look like in the future, but I cannot create the urgency to make changes. Look, change is hard. Most people are change averse, and often times it's just easier to keep doing what they're doing. If there isn't an emotional attachment to the problem, and a true desire to fix it, it's very unlikely that any changes will come from our work together.

That being said, it doesn't change the fact that you need a plan.

Think about it—if you were planning a vacation to Europe, when would you start planning the trip? The day before you leave? The week before? Of course not. That's a trip bound to cost much more than it should and will be full of stress and frustration. Most people plan vacations months or even years in advance, many times in great detail. Why would you do that? Because you want the trip to be enjoyable! The whole point of a vacation is to relax and have fun.

Yet research has shown that for a retirement journey that will last 15, 20, 30 years or more most people don't have an income plan. In fact, the most recent numbers I've seen show upwards of 70% of Americans have no income plan for retirement! Without an income plan, it's also likely that they have failed to consider the retirement risks that could be lurking around the corner as well.

This is a journey that has a much higher likelihood of failure and could mean stress, worry and doubt when it likely all could have been prevented with a good plan. As Winston Churchill famously said, "he who fails to plan is planning to fail."

How have you helped someone to overcome those obstacles, and what results were you able to gain for them?

Trust is by far the hardest obstacle to overcome because almost everyone has been burned by a financial professional in the past. They rightly bring that baggage with them to our relationship. Trust is really earned not by what you say but by what you do.

I tell all my clients that I appreciate that they have entrusted me with their finances, but I also tell them that the real proof is in the pudding. People can sense authenticity if you're candid with them. I don't want my clients ever to feel like I'm trying to sell them something because I'm not. In that way, I set myself apart from most other professionals in the industry.

I had an epiphany several years ago that came from the candid response of a client to a question I asked about why they decided to work with me. He said, "Bill, I've known for a while that having a plan is really important.

I have accumulated more than $2.5 million over the years. I've met with financial people like you before, but every time I did, I just felt intimidated and inadequate in understanding what they were explaining to me. So I just chose to go it alone." It was easier for him to put it aside and try to piece it together on his own because the intimidation he felt by a perceived financial information deficit was putting him in very real danger.

You see, planning is not enjoyable to most folks because, as advisors, we've created an environment that puts the client at an information disadvantage using confusing terminology and industry jargon. I think this has turned off a lot of good people from working with an advisor. Our income machines use clear, candid language and explain the planning process in terms that everyone can understand.

Some of the most satisfying outcomes are situations where people started the planning process and were certain they would never be able to retire. Most times, using their current angle of attack, they are right. Being able to show people where they are going if they continue with the status quo and how a properly managed plan can simply and easily change their course to one of financial success is truly rewarding.

What common misconceptions do your clients have around retirement planning?

While consulting with clients, the biggest misconception I find is assuming that having a financial advisor means having a financial plan. While these two concepts are not always mutually exclusive, far too many times they are! As a result, people continue down the road toward their retirement without actually knowing if they are going to end up where they desire to be.

Then there's the "big ugly hairy number" planning. This is the idea that you must grow your assets to a certain number, and as long as you only draw out a certain percentage each year in retirement, you'll be ok. But this is short-sighted because it's only a consumption plan. It fails to address the major retirement risks of inflation, market volatility, excess withdrawal, taxes, and longevity.

Anyone of these can totally derail even the best-laid plans. But set the risks aside for a moment. How do you know how much money you should save if you don't first know how much you're going to spend? Sure, it may be 10, 15 or 20 years away, but there are some very logical methods you can use to estimate your monthly or annual retirement expenses.

Another common obstacle to planning is the idea that you are immune to the things that can go wrong financially. In my experience, while people understand intellectually many things can go wrong over, let's say, a 30 year retirement period, most people believe that none of the things that *can* go wrong *will actually happen to them*. It's kind of a denial of reality, even though they are surrounded by people who run out of money, lose huge amounts of assets to nursing home care or other healthcare issues, pay too much in taxes, or don't compensate for the constant erosion of their dollars and purchasing power due to inflation.

Moreover, without a well-designed plan, when things change in the markets, the economy, or personal circumstances, people don't know what to do or are locked into a strategy which is no longer the best strategy for them.

We can't insulate our clients from everything that can go wrong. So we typically lay out the major retirement risks could hamper your retirement income plan. If the plan clearly provides the income you desire and cannot outlive, while also minimizing or eliminating inflation, income taxes, the sequence of investment returns, your chances of success just went up exponentially!

What unknown pitfalls should consumers be aware of when seeking financial guidance?

To be candid, I believe that consumers who are looking for financial guidance should be very cautious about with whom they choose to do business. That might seem like an obvious statement, but sometimes the dangers and pitfalls of working with the wrong person are hard to find.

Most financial professionals have a vested interest in selling a specific product, due to the fee or commission they will earn. Some are "captive" agents and can only sell certain products from certain companies. When you work for a company, there is always the corporate push for you to sell their products. It's difficult for those professionals to be holistic and objective in their choices on behalf of their clients and tend to recommend only the products and services, which they have to offer.

It's like going to a Toyota car dealership. Is the salesperson going to show you a Honda even if they think it might be in your best interests? Of course not! It's not in his interest to do so. So any financial planning structure where your interests are not primary is fraught with risks and dangers for you as the client. Remember, no product is perfect. Everything has pros and cons so if something sounds too good to be true, it probably is.

Seeking out an independent, fee-based fiduciary gives you, as the consumer, an advocate with the ability to shop for the very best solutions to your problem. In addition, it's critical to understand the pros and cons of any product, as well as the fee and commission structure so that you can provide clear "no" or "yes" answers in making your decisions.

Let me say a couple things about paying a fee for services. Some people might automatically think that paying a fee for a financial plan is a bad idea, but there is actually another side to the story. If the fee you are paying is to a fee-based fiduciary, then you are actually paying for their unbiased, holistic opinion. This is a benefit to you because you get to hear the pros and cons of products, not just the 'sizzle.' Just be careful with when the fee is collected. It's probably in your best interest to at least see if what you're trying to achieve matches up with the skill set of the advisor. Paying a fee upfront without this information might not truly empower you to properly 'interview' your new advisor.

Another thing to remember is that products do not equal a plan. While you will most certainly need specific products in order to create a plan, you have to be cautious of a financial advisor who leads with a product.

This is what I like to call "cart before the horse" financial planning. Imagine if you went to the doctor for a check-up because you weren't feeling well, and your doctor started prescribing medications before asking you any questions or even checking your vital signs! That is to say; a really good plan is one where you, along with the guidance of your advisor, are carefully crafting your ideal financial roadmap. Once your situation is properly diagnosed and the prognosis agreed upon, then and only then can the advisor coordinate with you to prescribe the solution and create your plan.

You are smart enough to create a successful retirement income plan, and with the right guidance, you'll be able to put the pieces in place for a successful journey.

What are some of your client's most common fears about financial planning?

Some of the fears clients experience are really simple, but not understanding them can completely derail your communication with people. At the beginning of my career, since I was younger than most of my clients, I thought I had to blow their hair back with my financial knowledge. Meetings that should only take an hour would drag on and on. And I couldn't understand why people weren't working with me.

It was a hard lesson to learn, but if you can't keep your word with something as simple as "the meeting will take an hour," you're sending the wrong message to the client. So I bought a time cube that rings after a specific period of time, at which point we end the meeting.

A second really big fear is what I like to call the time-share advisor. Clients are constantly worried that they are going to get trapped in an office until the advisor wears them down to the point of submission and they end up buying something that they're not really sure they need.

If this has ever happened to you before, you know how awful this feeling can be. Besides the negative feelings, this gives you, it also is a product first approach, which is *completely* out of sequence to true financial problem-solving. There are really about 5 or 6 steps that need to be in sequence before products are even discussed.

Another big issue is the "what's in it for him" problem. Again, early in my career, I was taught to really play up the sizzle of a product and avoid or downplay any negatives. While everyone feels great about the meeting, on the car ride home, the wife usually elbows her husband and says, "but what's in it for him"?

It wasn't until I realized that my job wasn't to sell but to educate that things began to change. My role as the advisor is to be truly unbiased and just present the pros and cons while your role as the client should be to simply provide clear "yes" and "no" on if they like the product. An advisor needs to be candid and transparent about the fees and commissions associated with any product.

A second issue which is virtually impossible to overcome is lack of emotion. People make decisions to change what they are currently doing when they realize the pain they are experiencing is intolerable and that they must do something about it. If that isn't apparent, then it's very unlikely any changes will be made.

Let's face it; change is hard. Most people are change averse, and it's just easier to keep doing what you've always been doing. So you're going to have to have some type of pain or fear that is intolerable that needs to be corrected NOW in order to act.

Why should your clients want to create a retirement income plan?

Merriam Webster's online version of their print dictionary defines the term "Stewardship" in the following way: *the conducting, supervising, or managing of something; especially: the careful and responsible management of something entrusted to one's care.* It has always been my personal view that our assets are a blessing from God and it is, therefore, incumbent on us to practice good stewardship over these blessings. Now, this is not to suggest in any way that if people aren't working with me, they aren't practicing good stewardship.

In fact, there are many times where a meeting will end with me saying, "I really think you're doing great where you are, and I don't think I can help you do any better."

However often times there are some very simple things that people can do to truly maximize their assets and enhance the performance of their current portfolio. Now *stewardship* might be considered a theological perspective, but it comes with a practical result.

You see one of the most enjoyable things I get to do every day with clients is showing them a picture of how things look currently versus how they might be improved by making some course corrections.

Often times the differences are vast and will allow people who never thought they could financially benefit future generations of their family be in a real position to do so.

I believe retirement should be the very best years of your life. Many people retire and have the world by the tail financially, only to make poor decisions and ruin it.

In that light I would say the most important thing you can do so that you can live out your life in peace and joy, is to surround yourself with a team of smart people who are dedicated to your guidance and success.

What led you to this field?

I grew up in the Charlotte metro area, so when the news came that our town was getting an NFL expansion team, I asked my dad if he would buy season tickets. My dad said he would be glad to buy a seat, as long as I was willing to earn money needed to buy my own seat. They cost $5,000 each, so I started my first business—cutting lawns. By the end of that summer, I had 30 clients and 4 people working for me. I had saved enough money to buy my Panthers PSL ticket (and a new set of wheels for my dad's mower). Of course, I learned the value of hard work, but also that there's a story behind your money.

Everyone who has built a 401k, IRA or stock account has a story behind their success which should also be listened to and be appreciated. You might just learn something!

Fast forward a few years to the business I now own and operate, Integrated Financial Concepts, LLC. Why am I a retirement income planner? Because I'm passionate about people and finances.

I believe that most people are inherently wise and understand they need a plan, a roadmap to follow. But their problem is that they just can't find an advisor in whom they trust, so they go without a plan. And unfortunately, they soon find out that traveling the retirement journey without a well-designed roadmap is not a good idea.

Money is important, but really, money is just fuel for your journey through life. Holistic planning ensures money is put to its highest and best use, which, in large part, will determine how enjoyable your journey will be.

I'm truly blessed to call myself a retirement income planner. What an awesome responsibility to help people be good stewards of the resources with which they have been blessed!

What are your final thoughts for consumers wanting to have a successful retirement?

We've been talking a lot about creating a plan. But really, you already have a plan. Think about that for a moment. Everyone *has* a plan. Even if you've never spent time putting a retirement income plan together, you have a plan. It just may not be a plan that's going to take you where you want to go.

Your retirement years should be some of the best of your life, so if you're not 100% sure where you stand, it's probably a good idea to get a second opinion. Hopefully, now you realize that not only do you need a plan, but you're empowered to find the right person to help you.

In the end, remember that while building a "retirement income machine" is important, of equal importance is finding someone you can ally with on your retirement journey.

A financial ally is a person you trust to call when the windy nights come and bumps in the road pop up on your journey.

You can do it! Keep your eyes and ears open while on your search and trust your instincts.

How can someone find out more about Bill Kearney and Integrated Financial Concepts, LLC and how you can help?

I'm happy to work with anyone who has a sincere willingness to do better than he or she is doing today and who, at the same time, has a willingness to change. It's interesting to me the number of people I have met who have huge financial problems but are not willing to change.

That's really hard for me. I know I can help them, but they are too afraid to change. They won't leave their comfort zone, even though that comfort zone is not working for their best interest.

Now, this is the point in the discussion where most financial professionals will try to manipulate, "find hot buttons," even beg to get the client to work with them. They try to "wow" the client through their knowledge-sharing and whiz-bang illustrations.

Almost always that leads to dissatisfaction with the results by the client and the advisor. It just shouldn't be that way, and so with me, it isn't that way. If you don't want to work with me, that's ok! And when I see you in the grocery store, you won't feel like you have to hide behind the meat counter to avoid me!

The best way to start a conversation is to call my office at 704.895.3003. If it makes sense to do so, we'll find a convenient time to sit down together in a free consultation and discuss your situation in more detail.

My website http://www.ifcadvisors.com is another great resource to learn more about my practice.

It's always my intent to go at your speed. If you decide to meet with me, our first meeting will just be a conversation.

We'll mostly just talk and answer questions, explain our process in more detail, and review some general ideas and strategies. There's absolutely no "sales pitch" or business transactions at this meeting.

ROCH TRANEL

CEO and Founder
The Tranel Financial Group

Email: rtranel@moneyconcepts.com
Website: www.tranelfinancial.com
LinkedIn: https://www.linkedin.com/in/rochtranel
Facebook: https://www.facebook.com/roch.tranel.9
Twitter: https://twitter.com/TranelFG
Call: (847) 680-9050

Roch Tranel, Certified Financial Planner, is CEO and founder of The Tranel Financial Group located in Libertyville, Illinois. Roch has been helping individuals reach clarity and confidence about their financial future for over 25 years.

Helping people *Enjoy a Better Life*™ through successful financial planning is Roch's passion in life. Roch has assembled a team of professional financial advisors who are committed to the same principles and share the same commitment to providing an unparalleled client experience.

As an active leader in his community, Roch has served on several boards, including the GLMV Chamber, The Rotary Club, and the Great Lakes Adaptive Sports Association and Pinnacle Forum. Currently, Roch is President of Founders 55 NFP, Inc. where he enjoys using his gifts of innovation and leadership.

He also shares these gifts by supporting The Global Leadership Summit, Freedom One Networking and the Taste of Life Program Intern Program at The Tranel Financial Group.

JORDAN BRADFORD

Financial Advisor
The Tranel Financial Group

Email: jbradford@moneyconcepts.com
Website: www.TranelFinancial.com
LinkedIn: www.linkedin.com/in/jordansbradford
Facebook: www.facebook.com/TheTranelFinancialGroup
Twitter: https://twitter.com/TranelFG
Call: (847) 680-9050

Jordan has an open and friendly demeanor which people naturally gravitate to. He is an enterprising advisor who listens intently to your needs and delivers the plan best suited to help you reach your financial goals.

His background in banking will help you navigate complex strategies and give you a fresh, innovative approach to understanding them.

Jordan has a Finance degree from Illinois Wesleyan University and is licensed with his Series 7, Series 66 and Life, Accident and Health Insurance. He is currently teaching the Dave Ramsey Financial Peace University class.

Jordan has a passion for politics, and in his free time he enjoys traveling, motorcycling, basketball, and any Chicago sports – Go Cubbies!

RETIRE COMFORTABLY AND STAY COMFORTABLY RETIRED
By Roch Tranel & Jordan Bradford

Describe the clients you work with and the types of situations they find themselves in when they come to you for your help?

Our clients are typically a married couple, usually between the ages of 50-65, who recognize that retirement is coming up around the corner and are looking for an independent voice to walk alongside them and help them to make the right financial decisions for their goals. These goals can vary quite drastically from client to client, but the root of their concern usually is founded in the following question...

Do I have enough money to retire comfortably and *stay* comfortably retired?

Completely answering that question is the driving force behind why our clients come to us and why they refer so many of their friends and family to us. This is answered simply by mapping out a solution that will show our clients where and how they will get their next paychecks in retirement. Not knowing what is next is a huge fear that everyone has leading up to retirement and the more we can plan for, the less we leave up to uncertainty.

Most of our clients share similarities in their reasoning for reaching out to us for help. As we near retirement, there are questions that we all have in our head. Some of those questions include: "What is my purpose now?", "Where will my next paycheck come from?", "How about leaving a Legacy?" and "What do I do if retirement is being forced on me?".

By answering these questions and putting together a roadmap for success, we are bringing clarity and confidence to our clients at a time when they may be struggling to find that in their life.

What common obstacles prevent your clients from staying comfortably retired?

Many people underestimate the importance of *staying* comfortably retired. Anyone can retire comfortably for some period, but the key to finding happiness and purpose in retirement is knowing that you can and will *stay* comfortably retired through the rest of your life.

One common obstacle that our clients face these days is the growing amount of debt that we carry with us. Debt can act as an anchor in retirement, keeping us in one place, and sometimes even pulling us underwater where we cannot survive. In our planning, debt management is the first conversation that we have. What many of our client's experience is that when your debt is under control, your freedom is increased substantially. Freedom to travel, freedom to spend your money, freedom to give, and freedom to leave a legacy are all impacted heavily by the amount of debt that we bring into retirement. The conversation about debt must happen early in the process in order for the rest of plan to work.

Another common obstacle that our clients must face is trying to keep up with their current lifestyle in retirement by taking in the same amount of income. This is one that almost everyone has in common. When you make $100,000 working, you expect to make $100,000 in retirement to live the same lifestyle. After all, you will now have all this free time available because you are not working so we figure our expenses will at the very least stay the same, if not increase.

While it is true in many cases that you will have more expenses early on in retirement as you cross off some of those bucket list items (traveling, a new car, vacation home, etc.), there are many expenses that we no longer have (mortgage, car payment, 401(k) contributions, etc.). If you do have some of these going into retirement, what we must do is put together a plan that gives you the freedom to accomplish your goals and still take care of your financial obligations.

The third obstacle that many people have in *staying* comfortably retired is planning for healthcare costs. The reason this is so common nowadays is that people are living longer than ever before.

This means that not only does your money need to last longer for your life, but many of our clients end up having to take care of their parents, which can be an added cost in retirement if the parents did not plan well. So, as people live longer, we must be prepared for the possibility that we may end up having to take care of a sick spouse or parent and paying for the cost, out of pocket. Our unique income solutions help our clients understand and prepare for these costs that will come up.

Share a few examples of how you would help your clients to overcome obstacles, and what kind of results you'd be able to gain for them?

When in the process of helping our clients prepare for retirement, we utilize a unique strategy that we developed and fine-tuned over the years that we call the Growth and Income Strategy, which can be found in our book, "Sunny Side Up." This strategy is unique in that it is designed to address our client's obstacles and challenges that keep them from retiring comfortably and staying comfortably retired.

Our Life Enjoyment Experience is the unique process by which we guide our clients to their goals and continue to walk with them throughout the rest of their lives. This involves regular account review meetings that we refer to as our Faithful Watch Process. This is an important step in our process for the clients because we use these meetings to help instill clarity and confidence in what we have set out to accomplish for each and every client.

First, we address the debt that our clients have currently, and we learn more about the history of that debt and determine how long it will take to pay down if we do nothing differently. Many situations we come across involve clients having a mortgage, car payment, and some level of credit card debt or student loan debt that they are paying on behalf of themselves or their children. Using the debt snowball strategy that has been made popular by Dave Ramsey, we look to the different ways we can accelerate paying that debt off, or at the very least, making it more manageable. We always come up with a solution to this before moving to the next step.

Next, we evaluate our client's spending habits. Our goal is not to reduce the amount of money that our clients spend or change their lifestyle going into retirement. We simply want to understand what is most important to our clients, so we can design a plan that helps them to reach those specific goals. Because leading up to retirement can be a scary time, we use the Growth and Income Strategy to map out the cash flow necessary for our clients to maintain their lifestyle. By breaking up their retirement into the many different time horizons that are to come, we can accurately plan for what we will need to spend and how that money will be generated.

A notable example of a time horizon is the time between where you are at now and when you intend to retire. This is not your only time horizon, but it is typically the first one that is planned out. The next time horizon could be from your retirement date until you begin taking social security. These different time horizons must be mapped out so that we can adequately allocate your retirement cash flow.

What are some of your client's most common misconceptions about Financial Services?

Being Independent Financial Planners is something that many of our clients have never heard of before they sit down with us for the first time. While many financial advisors work for large warehouse firms, we at The Tranel Financial Group are completely independent. That is so important for clients these days because it means that we do not work for a specific investment company.

We do not have proprietary products that we are selling, nor do we have a one-size-fits-all approach to investing. Our independence allows us to sit on the same side of the table as our clients to be a non-biased advocate on their behalf. We research the best investments available and put together a customized solution based on our client's specific needs.

Another common misconception that comes up often is that people may not understand the difference between a fee-based advisor and one that is commission based. However, there is a stark difference between the two ways that Financial Institutions make money.

Commission based advising is the way most financial planners have operated historically. How this works is that whenever a client needs to buy or sell any investments, the advisor charges a commission to place the trade or change the investment. These commissions can cost clients up to 5.75% of their investment.

Where the problem really comes up is when a commission based advisor recommends buying or selling something, they are getting paid to do so. As you can see, the advisor can make large commissions on their clients, while the client's investments could be stagnant or even losing money.

Fee-based advising is the way that we, as advisors, act in a fiduciary capacity. Fee-based advising means that there are no commissions charged, just a small quarterly fee to manage investments, and when our clients do well, we do well. There are never any commissions, so our clients know that our recommendations are free from any conflicts of interest. Being a fiduciary means that we are required to act in our client's best interest. While this may seem obvious, it is important to ask your advisor if they are a fiduciary and if so, how do they get paid.

Lastly, we still find many people who believe that they do not have enough money to work with a financial advisor. This simply could not be further from reality. While many companies may target to specific demographics and only work with minimum account sizes, our independent company works with clients of all sizes.

We pride ourselves on serving our clients regardless of what investments they have, and because we are fee-based, we can charge for our services appropriately, instead of forcing clients to pay large commissions if they don't meet certain minimums.

What pitfalls or mistakes should your clients be aware of?

People have a strong tendency to overestimate things that have a low probability of happening and underestimate things with a high probability of happening. Studies show people are willing to go to extreme lengths to prevent getting sick from diseases that they have a less than 5% chance of ever contracting, including spending countless time, energy, and money to fight.

However, when presented with a potential disease that we have a 50% chance of developing, we are unwilling to go to the same lengths to reduce our chances of this disease. This is fascinating because we are far more likely to get the disease in my second example, however, because we do underestimate this scenario, we are not likely to spend our money to prevent this.

The same is true with our money. Clients know that taxes and inflation will impact retirement but rarely is that something that people want to plan for. Taxes and inflation are known in the industry as the twin destroyers of wealth. They get this name because if we are not prepared for their effect, we will lose out on a lot of our retirement assets.

Healthcare and Social Security are other notable examples. Studies show that the clear majority of Americans have little to no money set aside for future healthcare expenses, nor are they adequately insured for Long-Term Care, even though statistically nearly 70% of retirees will need Long-Term Care at some point in their life. This would be an example of underestimating a high probability event.

On the flip side, many people believe that they will not receive Social Security and they don't want to plan on getting it. Realistically speaking, the probability that someone who is turning 65 this year will not receive Social Security benefits they are entitled to is about as close to 0% as you can get. Due to our overreaction, though, we believe this is something we need to plan for while leaving our Long-Term Care, unfunded.

What are your client's most common fears about retirement planning?

Surprisingly enough, many people are not convinced that a retirement plan will work for them. We often hear people say that their situation is so unique, that no one else could help them. The reality is that we have a great deal of experience customizing tailored plans for our clients and the chances are very high that we have seen a case like yours before and we are well prepared to find you a solution.

"Will I outlive my money?"

This is a very common question that we get. When you retire, you have two doors to go through. Through door number one, your money outlives you. Through door number two, you outlive your money. There is no in between here. This is a fear that we can all relate to because, at the end of the day, it is the most important question to answer when planning your retirement.

Having someone look through all your finances can feel very intimate. When you sit down with someone that you may not know, it can be intimidating, and often we hear people tell us they are embarrassed by how much they have saved up or that they feel should know more. There is never any reason to be embarrassed.

When you go to the doctor, it is important to tell them everything that is going on with your body, so they can give you the right prescription. The good doctors do not judge you for where you are at, and good financial advisors are the same way. We want to know everything possible simply so that we can provide you with a valuable plan that can be followed.

Why would your clients want to retire comfortably and stay comfortably retired?

This is probably the most obvious question because everyone wants to retire and *stay* comfortably retired. When our clients achieve this goal, they gain peace of mind, clarity and confidence, and financial independence.

One example that comes to mind embodies these goals. We had a client come to us through a referral of an existing client that was impressed with the work that we do. She was recently widowed and had worked for one company for many years. As she approached retirement, she leaned on the advice of a friend, who suggested she meet with their financial planner to help her navigate.

When we sat down, we quickly discovered that there were some complexities in her life. She had a company 401(k) plan, stock options, a pension plan, life insurance, and a few other assets. Before her husband had passed, he managed all their finances, including setting up life insurance to help pay off the debt that remained on the house. It was clear that he had planned well, but this lady who came to us did not know if she was in good standing or not.

What we helped her do was to get everything organized in her life. We used out white walls in our office to draw a picture of what her retirement looks like. She loved this, as many clients do. We made a complex situation seem simple to her. There were many moving parts. We had to set up trusts and consolidate accounts that were set up at various companies over the years. She had peace of mind knowing that we could help her make sense of everything.

Our ability to simplify her complexities was what she really loved about working with us. Because of the work that did, she was able to retire comfortably, and she has financial independence, clarity, and confidence. These things are crucial to maintaining a successful retirement.

When you know that your money will outlive you, you are able to live and give like no one else. The independence that a successful retirement brings about can be incredibly powerful. We want all our clients to experience the pure joy of being able to enjoy their retirement the way they have always envisioned. Your goals can be accomplished, and you can know, confidently, that you will be better than ok, your retirement will be amazing!

What led you to this field?

I have always had a passion for helping people achieve success. I absolutely love being able to make a positive difference in someone's life, and through our work at The Tranel Financial Group, I can do that each and every day.

Roch Tranel, our CEO, and Founder has done an excellent job in sharing his vision for a bright future with me and because of the mentoring and guidance that I have received from him, I have been able to channel that vision and deliver it to our clients.

Roch started The Tranel Financial Group in 1988 with the help of his wife, Kat. Since then, the company has grown into a multi-advisor business that consistently delivers a high standard of excellence.

Our passion for delivering clarity and confidence through excellent service can be seen not only in our client relations that we have developed but through our community involvement. We live out our values every day in the ways in which we give back to our community here in Lake County. It is that mindset that keeps me so passionate about the excellent work we do for our clients.

Please share your final thoughts for anyone wanting to retire comfortably and stay comfortably retired?

You only get one chance to crack open your retirement nest egg, and it is essential that you are well positioned for your retirement. So much can happen in your life once you retire, that having a financial advisor who is also an advocate for you can be the difference maker in your success. We often recommend that people interview multiple financial advisors before they select one because everyone has different strategies. Retirement is only the first step in the client relationship.

Our job as financial advisors to be right there with you over the next 30 years, helping you make the right decisions and getting your money to work just as hard for you as you had to work for it. Above all, however, the most important piece of advice that we have for you is to have a plan. Even a plan that isn't perfect is better than no plan at all when entering retirement.

If the reader wants to know more, how can they connect with you?

We offer many ways for people to connect with us for free. If you go to our website, www.thetranelfinancialgroup.com, you can take our key question quiz to determine how much money you need to retire.

With that information, we also offer a free complimentary one-on-one meeting where we can answer any questions and evaluate your current situation to see how we can help.

Our website also has many other resources such as our other books, "Sunny Side Up," "Eight Things I Wish I Knew Before I Retired," and "The Friend Economy." These books address different facets of our business, who we are, and what value we bring.

If you are reading this and want to speak with someone directly, you can call us at 847-680-9050 to set up a complimentary meeting. Our first step is to take you through our Life Enjoyment Process, beginning with what we call the Discovery meeting.

This meeting is best described as a date without the awkwardness. It is an opportunity for us to get to know you and for you to get to know us, so we can determine how we fit in your life.

We really look forward to the opportunity to bring value to your life and help you retire comfortably and stay comfortably retired.

JONATHAN P. McCORMICK

Enrolled Agent, M.S. Taxation
Hillhurst Tax Group

Email: JM@HillhurstTaxGroup.com
Website: www.HillhurstTaxGroup.com
Office Direct: (818) 337-5233
Office Main: (323) 210-8102

After earning his Bachelor's Degree in Psychology from Kansas Wesleyan University, Jonathan returned home to California to begin his career in Taxation. After years of work experience in the field, he completed the Master of Science Program in Taxation at California State University, Northridge.

Practicing as an Enrolled Agent, Jonathan works directly with taxpayers and the IRS collection division every day. Over the past 6 years, he has saved his clients millions of dollars through compromised settlements with the IRS.

Many others have seen their tax liens released, wage garnishments or bank levy removed, and/or audits balances drastically reduced.

Favorite Color: Green. **Favorite Hobby**: Soccer

IRS TAX DEBT RELIEF
RETIRE WITH PEACE OF MIND
By Jonathan P. McCormick

Describe the clients you work with and the types of situations they find themselves in when they come to you for your help?

We help taxpayers in collections owing $10,000 or more in IRS tax debt to reduce their IRS tax debt when possible, so they can have peace of mind when dealing with the IRS tax debt. Our clients usually receive a collection notice or set of notices from the IRS via regular or certified mail. Some clients receive a notice for the balance due.

These clients likely already filed and owed taxes and never paid the balance due. Others receive a notice they are being audited, or the IRS already audited and is making changes to their tax return, resulting in a tax balance due. Some clients are even waiting until the bank account is levied or their paycheck is garnished before deciding to seek help.

These clients usually get the notice from their bank branch or employer after the IRS has started collecting. We help clients at all stages of the IRS collection process.

Knowing what stage of collections the case is in helps our clients receive some immediate peace of mind, even before starting to work with us on their tax debt relief.

What common obstacles prevent your clients from having peace of mind when dealing with the IRS?

One common obstacle that prevents our clients from having peace of mind when dealing with the IRS is the horror stories they may hear from friends or family regarding the IRS. Taxes a private matter for most people and they are likely not disclosing full details to you when they share their experiences in dealing with the IRS.

Many times taxpayers compare someone else's situation to their own when in the collection department each taxpayer is reviewed on a case-by-case basis. Income, assets, and circumstances differ from taxpayer to taxpayer, so it's difficult to know exactly how your result compares to the result of a friend or family member.

Another common obstacle the prevents our clients from having peace of mind when dealing with the IRS is that the IRS is not an easy place to communicate with. When calling by phone, taxpayers usually experience multiple menus and voice prompts, along with minutes to hours of hold time, depending on the day.

Many times the answer the taxpayer needs can't be resolved in one phone call, and a follow-up call is required. The pattern continues unless the taxpayer and IRS reach an agreement. Many taxpayers don't have the free time to dedicate multiple days and hours calling the IRS to reach a resolution.

When sending a fax to the IRS, the response takes about 2-4 weeks and will likely come via mail, adding another week to arrive. When sending mail to the IRS, the response almost always takes 30 days or more. The response will also be via mail. If the desired result is not reached, taxpayers find themselves frustrated at the lack of progress and time required to continue working to reach their result.

Another common obstacle that prevents our clients from having peace of mind when dealing with the IRS is the fear to ask for help. Many clients know they have a tax debt problem and know they will deal with it next week, next month, next year, etc.

Once it gets put off for too long, the problem becomes less important because it's been put off for this long, why not a little longer? Eventually, the collection action begins, and a pay-check is being garnished, or a bank account is being levied.

The fear of another pay-check garnishment or bank levy is tough to remove from most taxpayer's minds. Having the proper help, and being comfortable asking for the help, can keep the peace of mind now and in the future.

How would you go about helping someone to achieve peace of mind when dealing with the IRS, and what kind of results would you typically be able to gain for them?

To help clients achieve peace of mind when dealing with the IRS, we ask them to contact us first by phone, so we can decide where the case is at and how we are able to move forward. Usually, clients call once they have a received a notice of balance due, notice of tax lien or levy, or notice of tax return audit from the IRS. Sometimes clients receive just one notice and have an issue for one tax year, but many times clients receive multiple notices for multiple tax years. Clients will bring those notices to our office and complete a brief questionnaire either before the appointment or during the office visit.

We may ask for some financial documents as well to help give a more thorough initial case review. Even clients without notice copies or financial documents can begin the questionnaire and give us an idea of how the problem started.

Finally, we compare our client's notices along with their income, expenses, assets, and equity to the IRS national standards to make sure we are able to assist before moving forward.

Clients then sign a tax specific limited Power of Attorney, Form 2848, giving our representative the ability to communicate with the IRS on behalf of the client. From that point forward, the IRS is no longer allowed to contact our client without first contacting us. Any notices mailed will be copied to our office as well.

Filing Form 2848 is an important first step in giving our clients peace of mind. Most taxpayers qualify for one of the fresh start programs offered by the IRS; the next step is deciding which program is best for them.

To decide the best program, we prepare IRS Form 433-A based on the information provided to us. This form helps determine the amount of monthly disposable income available to the client as well as an equity in assets.

The IRS views monthly disposable income and equity as collection potential for taxpayers. Clients with little to no monthly disposable income are often candidates for the Offer In Compromise program, designed to reduce the tax debt based on collection potential and ability to repay the debt over time. This is the program most clients want to qualify for, as it will reduce debt significantly.

Clients with higher monthly disposable income also qualify for this program, but they will settle at a higher amount than someone with little to no monthly disposable income.

For Ronald, Annette, Ernest, and Jose, we were able to show the IRS no disposable monthly income to pay back towards the debt. Once we substantiate the income and assets to the IRS, they are willing to settle debts for incredibly low amounts.

Ronald owed over $8,000 to the IRS and Annette over $20,000; both settled for $100.

Ernest owed over $25,000 and settled for $1,600. Ernest would have also settled at $100, but he had an extra old motorcycle worth $1,600, which IRS views as equity he can use to pay towards the debt. He was still happy to pay the $1,600 on his debt of over $25,000.

Jose had a debt of over $5,000 to the IRS and settled for just $50!

When the information is presented to the IRS correctly and completely, the results that follow are often extremely positive for our clients.

For Scottie, Nathan, and Frank, we were able to show the IRS although they had some monthly disposable income, as well as some equity in assets, was not enough to ever pay their debt over time.

Scottie owed more than $300,000 to the IRS and settled for $24,852. Scottie had some disposable monthly income and a retirement account with equity that was used to pay towards his settlement.

Nathan owed more than $90,000 to the IRS and settled for $7,828. Nathan had disposable monthly income of over $500/month.

Frank owed more than $700,00 and settled for $13,692. Frank had a closed business with significant outstanding debt, as well as personal tax debt. His monthly disposable income was over $1,000/month and was still able to settle for $13,692.

Scottie was a special case for us, as he had tried this program on his own and with a different representative with no success. He came to us after his 2nd attempt was rejected by the IRS. We had 30 days to appeal when he contacted us for help.

Within that time frame, we were able to submit a timely appeal and have the IRS review his income and expenses again, as they had disallowed a number of his expenses that he provided substantiation for already. After two readjustments of his financial information, the IRS determined that they could accept his offer if he paid $24,852.

We helped Scottie avoid having to submit a third offer while giving peace of mind and restored confidence, not only in the IRS but in himself and his future as well.

What common misconceptions may your clients have about reducing IRS tax debt?

The most common misconception clients have about reducing their IRS tax debt is thinking the program won't apply to their situation. Clients hear about settlements on TV advertisements and radio regarding "settle for pennies on the dollar," and think it is too good to be true when in reality, they are happening for our clients every month. Many people feel those advertisements are scams to get them to call in. As long as you call the right person, there is no reason to worry.

Another common misconception for clients is they think this process is going to take too long or be too complicated for them. The process, once you know where to start, is often very similar for every taxpayer.

Although each client's case may start at a different spot in the collection, once that is determined there are not many surprised or factors that can cause a client's case to change course. Most clients are not aware of the allowable expenses and exemptions the IRS gives to taxpayers when trying to reduce their debt.

What should people be aware of when evaluating a tax professional's services?

The tax relief industry has a reputation that many good tax professionals suffer from, which is a reputation of charging fees, high fees, and often for a service, the taxpayer does not qualify for, leaving clients out of lots of money with no IRS resolution. When contacting a professional for help with the IRS collections, not just any tax professional is experienced in the IRS collections procedures.

The majority of tax professionals and accounting firms do not work with IRS collections on a daily basis. You want to make sure that the company you hire is specializing in IRS collection cases. You also want a company that can show you prior client results similar to your own situation.

When hiring a professional in the IRS tax debt field, a good question to start with is "are you the person who will be working on my case?"

Many times you will not speak to the person representing you, especially if you have your initial consultation over the phone. The person speaking to you may be selling you a dream story, but he is not the person performing any of this work he is telling you about.

It is important to ask to speak to the licensee who will be handling your case, as they are the person who communicates directly with the IRS.

If the person you speak with is not licensed and does not offer you a chance to meet with or speak to your licensee, this is a red flag. Unless the licensee is busy at the moment, they'll often be able to greet you and let you know they'll be the person working on your case.

Experience is another important thing to look for when choosing a representative. You may want to ask questions like "how many installment agreements have you submitted recently?" or "how many offers in compromises have you had accepted recently?" or "how did the audit go for your last client?".

These questions relate to the specific programs available to taxpayers with IRS tax debt. Those who are not able to answer questions like this may not be doing the type of work you need on a regular basis. They may still be a competent tax professional, but not experienced in the IRS collections process and procedures.

Something else to look out for are low start-up fees, usually leading to a very steep second charge or up-sale. If you don't pay the second large fee, your case will be closed, and you won't be refunded your original startup cost.

There are many stories of taxpayers hiring a company for an initial flat fee, assuming it covers their entire case, only to find out later that they need to pay more fees, usually significantly more than they've already paid, to continue with the help they need. This is how the industry gained such a poor reputation.

What are your client's most common fears about even attempting to get IRS tax debt help?

The most common fears for clients when deciding whether or not they should start getting help often involves how do they pick the right person to help them and how much it is going to cost them. After clients meet us for the first time, the fear of who to pick is taken care of.

When worried about the amount of fees, we are often not the cheapest option but never the most expensive. We offer many payment options for clients, with most of our clients having a unique payment structure for their services.

Each client comes to us with a unique financial situation, so we try to structure their payments to us that way as well, easing any worries of having to come up with something that they do not have.

Another common fear for clients is not being convinced that the programs will work for them. It is easy to think the results on advertisements are all "too good to be true" or "that won't apply to me."

What clients don't know is that there are programs for taxpayers in all ranges of tax debts and who receive different types of notices. The IRS has set up programs for clients between $0-$10,000, $10,000 - $25,000, $25,000-$50,000, $50,000-$100,000, and taxpayers over $100,000 in tax debt.

Each program is unique to the debt amount, and taxpayers can qualify for different programs as their debt amounts change. Just because the advertisement or example client is not an exact reflection of their situation, doesn't mean that there is not an IRS program available to them.

It sounds obvious, but why would your clients want to reduce their IRS tax debt?

Clients want to reduce their IRS tax debt for different reasons, but none more than to have peace of mind when living their day-to-day life. Clients have shared stories about their IRS tax debt issue as something that has lingered for weeks, months, or even years before deciding to face the problem.

Most clients are so relieved when the process is complete; they have to learn how to live their life again without the burden of the IRS weighing down on them. Some simply want to avoid accruing new interest and new penalty fees. These clients seem to contact us as soon as they receive a notice from the IRS, rather than letting the problem sit unresolved.

More specifically, clients ready to start a new life by getting married want to be sure they clear their IRS tax debt, so it doesn't burden their new spouse. Although IRS tax debt for one spouse will never be owed by the new spouse, finances are usually jointly managed after marriage and for one spouse to have an IRS tax debt can put a huge burden on the relationship. Lots of our clients who are married and had a debt prior to marriage want to reduce their IRS tax debt simply to ease the burden on their new spouse and their marriage.

Other clients want to reduce their IRS tax debt because they need to qualify for financing, usually to find a new home or new vehicle. Clients can get a home or vehicle with outstanding IRS tax debt, but if the IRS files a tax lien, it makes financing more difficult, sometimes impossible.

The IRS programs are designed to help clients release their tax liens to qualify for housing and vehicle financing. Also, clients who may need to refinance their home have a program available for them too. Our clients are usually extremely satisfied when they are able to purchase their new home, new vehicle, or refinance their current mortgage without the IRS tax debt holding them back.

What led you to this field?

I originally began my career in IRS tax debt relief because of a financial need instead of a want. My mother passed away in 2011, and I was forced to move home to California from Kansas, where I had just graduated college and started working using my degree in psychology.

After a few weeks at home, a longtime friend of our family offered me a position working for a tax relief company. After a few months, I was able to move into the resolution department and could show my skills and work ethic, although I had no experience with taxes at the time. One of the enrolled agents at the firm saw my potential and decided to take me under her wing.

If it wasn't for this person, I would not be where I am today. She pushed me to study and become licensed myself, knowing full well that I could represent clients and be successful in this industry. Due to my fragile emotional state losing my mother, I was fully focused on making this person proud of investing their time in me.

Within 9 months I had gone from a telemarketer making outbound calls to prospective clients, to a licensed Enrolled Agent, representing some of the biggest clients and cases at the firm. I chose to specialize in the IRS fresh start program, and have not looked back since.

After gaining some work experience as a licensed enrolled agent, the same person pushed me to further my education by going back to school. I applied and was accepted to the Masters in Science Taxation program at California State University Northridge. I was the youngest student in my cohort and was the least experienced tax professional the program had ever accepted, especially since my undergraduate degree was in psychology and not accounting like the vast majority of the other students.

Upon completion of the program, I was one of the top 10 students in my cohort. I was also able to run the low-income tax clinic for a year and was presented with an outstanding service award and scholarship during the graduation ceremony, a complete surprise to my family and I that day.

Upon receiving my Masters degree, I started my own company, Hillhurst Tax Group, and have been assisting taxpayers with IRS tax debt ever since. We have built our brand over the last 3 years as one of the most highly rated tax relief firms in Los Angeles.

We get such high-quality results because we have built rapport with the many of the IRS offer examiners, revenue agents, and revenue officers, and our internal systems have been streamlined to mimic the IRS for maximum quality and efficiency.

What are your final thoughts for the reader who wants to reduce their IRS tax debt and have peace of mind when dealing with the IRS?

For clients who want to reduce their IRS tax debt and have peace of mind when dealing with the IRS, contacting us will save them time, save them money, and save them worry. Our prices may not be the lowest priced relief company out there, but we are not the most expensive.

Most clients feel our fees are worth the results they get to take home with them. When we meet with prospective clients, we only take the case if we are very confident of meeting their expectations. Our clients see such positive results because we set realistic expectations up front, and deliver results on those expectations we promised.

Our fees are often customized client by client, based on your specific financial situation right now. We do this because clients with IRS tax debt are often facing financial difficulties and we don't want the price to be a reason that they continue to have IRS tax debt if we know we can get them a successful result.

Also, it only takes one phone call or one office visit to get us started on your case. Usually, in a 30-60 minute consultation, we can review your notices, your tax returns, your financial documents, and provide you with a detailed action plan for moving forward. After that initial meeting, the only time required from our clients is when we need signatures, brief explanations, or to answer any questions or concerns of the clients on what is happening now and what happens next.

For clients who think they can do it themselves, we usually offer as much free advice as possible before wishing them luck on their own. We always provide our contact information for emergencies in the future.

About 1 in 3 clients who contact us first and don't sign up end up calling us back because they found it too difficult to do on their own or found that the person they chose to hire was not the right choice. These clients are always long lasting clients because the quality of service and results we provide is often tough to duplicate.

If the reader wants to know more, how can they connect with you?

To get more information about Hillhurst Tax Group and peace of mind when dealing with the IRS, you should visit our website at http://www.hillhursttaxgroup.com and read some of the reviews and testimonials from our clients that have already experienced successful results. It is likely that one of those reviews will relate to your situation.

Our website also has videos explaining how the process works at our firm, as well as how the IRS collections department works.

We offer a free tax relief consultation either via phone or in person. We only take cases that we know we can help, which is why our success rate and positive rating has stayed so high for so long. Although we prefer our clients to meet us face-to-face, we service clients nationwide and are able to provide full service via phone, email, and fax.

To set up a phone or in person consultation, we encourage you to call us at (323) 486-3314.

You will likely speak to a case manager or tax associate when you call in. This person will take your general information and set up your consultation or phone appointment.

KATHRYN AMENTA

Kathryn Amenta, Money Coach
San Francisco, CA

Email: kathryn@kathrynamenta.com
Website: http://www.kathrynamenta.com
LinkedIn: http://linkedin.com/in/kathrynamenta
Facebook: www.facebook.com/kathrynamentamoneycoach
Twitter: https://twitter.com/kathrynamenta
Call: (415) 519-3013

Kathryn Amenta helps individuals and couples master money in their lives. She is able to do so because she has done it in her own life. Kathryn has developed a masterful process for coming to grips with the emotions underlying your money problems, and a protocol for tracking and analyzing your cash flow based on criteria aligned with your true needs and life purpose.

Her process stems from degrees in psychology and finance, work in the corporate financial industry, and the deep, continuous healing of her own money problems. Her process is life transforming. She works globally from her base in San Francisco, CA.

BECOME A MASTER OF YOUR MONEY AND YOUR LIFE
By Kathryn Amenta

Tell us about Kathryn Amenta, Money Coach, the individuals and couples you work with and the types of situations they find themselves in when they come to you for your help?

I am a money coach, and I offer a specialized and individualized process that helps people overcome their money problems. This is much different from other financial approaches that focus entirely on creating a budget.

A budget *can be* an effective money tracking tool--but ONLY IF it goes hand-in-hand with uncovering and transforming the emotions fueling the spending and debting behaviors that have caused your problems and brought pain and suffering in your life.

My process, as a Money Coach, goes to the root of your money problems.

- What are your internal messages about money?

- What do you tell yourself about your worth in the world?

- What are the emotional triggers that feed your spending behaviors?

- What do you believe money should do for you in life?

- How do you feel inside when money problems sabotage what you want and think you deserve in life?

Many people are in deep emotional pain and suffering about their money--and their lives. Many are fighting about money within themselves and with the people in their relationships. Fighting about money in the relationship is one of the big issues that bring people to my door.

My process is effective for individuals and couples from all income levels: people who have wealth and people with modest means. They cover a wide age range—young adults to retirees.

They come to me because they are fighting about money, choking in debt and think there is no way out. They have a lot of conflicted emotions about money and confusion, mostly stemming from what they learned in their families of origin and cues from the society.

They have great shame about their money problems, fear of failure, and fear that if anyone finds out, they will be deemed horribly unworthy of love and acceptance. Some are going through major life changes, like a divorce, and have never handled money on their own.

Some are on the brink of entering a committed relationship and need help talking together about money. Many fear they will never have enough money to be able to retire. Fear of money can be almost as strong as fear of death.

What are the advantages of replacing shame and fear with mastery?

What is shame? Paraphrasing Dr. Brene Brown, shame is an intensely painful and paralyzing emotion that makes us feel we are flawed and unworthy of love, connection, and belonging. Don't be fooled; there is nothing noble or productive about shame. It is caustic.

Shame stops us dead in our tracks and makes us want to hide away behind dark curtains. It is based on the belief that if anyone found out the truth about your money problems they'd know you are not good enough. This describes most everyone on the planet today, to some degree.

We all suffer from some degree of shame about how much we have, how much we don't have and the debt collectors nipping at our heels.

But the reality is, for many of us, money problems stem from our lack of money knowledge. Appropriate money skills were not the curriculum in our schools, and sadly not in our families.

Often our money problems can be traced back many generations. They are also the product of our religious and cultural institutions and age-old social taboos. It is only when we bring our money problems into the light of day and admit to them that real--life transforming--change can happen.

What do you feel are the biggest myths when it comes to money behavior?

A very prevalent myth is that we must always wear a "good face" in the world. We must always give the impression that says we know exactly what we are doing with our money, and that we are competent. We live in a world that rewards us for saying that we are masters of our lives. In doing so, we get cut off from our true feelings.

Another myth and it goes hand in hand with the first, is that we have to buy the latest fashion, the hottest technology, dine at the trendiest restaurants and have all the other trappings of a glamorous lifestyle, regardless of whether we can actually pay for it and how much debt it causes.

Still another myth is that the more money we have, the less we have to pay attention to it. This goes together with the notion that if you have a problem, you can just throw money at it.

What are the common misconceptions about the financial industry?

We want to trust that people in power have our best interests at heart. So we want to believe that people and institutions in the financial industry are looking out for our best financial outcome. This could not be further from the truth. Many financial institutions and the people who work for them are only incentivized to be concerned with the interest of their shareholders and making commissions. They are also much more concerned with supporting the interests of the big fish, and have little or no incentive to be interested in the lives of the "Common Joe."

What are some common fears about finance?

Let's start by defining "fear." Fear is an emotional, psychological or physical feeling of pain associated with a sense of impending doom. Fear hits you in the core of your gut. When it comes to their money, most people fear others will find out about their real money situation and discover they are frauds in this charade that they are competent worthy individuals.

Another fear is that we are not worthy human beings, and are not good enough to manage money ourselves. Deep down, we feel lonely and afraid for our survival. Most of us have a deep, and often unexpressed desire, to have someone else take care of us and our money.

What can the individuals and couples you work with do to get past those fears?

The important step is bringing fear into the light, so you can look it in the face, dissect it to see where it stems from and why it arises. My process reveals the true face of your fear, so you can step outside it and lessen its grip on you. We look at your money backstory and the emotions that drive the behaviors that result in your money problems. With this incremental process, most people can change.

It is always a question of whether you are willing to do the work. Are you willing to stop listening to the old tapes, incorporate new ideas and learn new skills? Are you ready to recognize and work through your fears with someone you can trust?

Once you lay your problems on the table, you can gain clarity and begin to move on. But you have to be willing to show up, to want to succeed, and to take the time and effort necessary. You also have to be willing to be patient and accepting of yourself, even at the times when you slip back into old behaviors.

What other perceived obstacles might be preventing people from seeking the help of a Money Coach?

There are certain families and "tribes" of people that think it is shameful to open up and share your problems with strangers. Since you are expected to be competent, if you need to ask for help, this must be a sign of your weakness. And, even if deep down you want to change your money behaviors and are willing to do the work and believe you deserve more, you may still allow pressure from family and friends to hold you back. You can fear the loss of family and friends who will say to you, "You think you're better than me."

When it comes to replacing shame and fear with mastery, what are some of the common pitfalls you see individuals and couples of all ages make?

Lack of motivation and fear of failure are the big pitfalls. It takes commitment to doing the work and staying the course to bring about success. Your problems, coupled with trouble in the world can make it seem very overwhelming. But you just keep at it, step by step, believing that you deserve more in your money and your life. You may also still think you are not able to change or not good enough to change, so why even try.

For couples, each person has to be willing to work with the other's emotional baggage—that bag of rocks we all carry on our shoulders. You don't have to resonate with your partner's problems, but you have to be willing to work with each other.

Each of you grew up with and operates from a different set of money rules. Your money rocks don't come from the same quarry. And if the relationship is problematic, to begin with, pushing the money issues could cause you to fall apart.

Finally, most of us have resistance to change, to some degree. We want to keep our lives stable and predictable, even if our money life is dysfunctional.

How can these pitfalls be avoided?

You always have to be willing to step out of your comfort zone to affect real change. That means slowing down and looking at the habitual ways you have used money. It means setting up new criteria for yourself about what you purchase and why.

Instead of automatically making a purchase, give yourself some space to evaluate whether that purchase is really good for you based on that new criteria. Understand the pros and cons of the purchase decision.

Ask: "Why am I interested in this? How will it benefit my real needs?" That purchase may soothe you immediately, but will it bring lasting value to your life? Think it through, and connect with the feelings behind your desire to purchase something.

Share an example of how you've helped someone to overcome obstacles and succeed in making their own powerful money decisions.

I work with a well-educated teacher at a top-ranked school. Growing up, her parents had terrible money problems and did not provide well for her needs. So she adopted the belief that she needed a partner to take care of her because she was not good enough to do it alone.

I am supporting her in changing the messages in her head with the mantra: "I am doing a good job, and I am working hard at it." She is beginning to operate also from the understanding that she is not a perfect human being and she will make mistakes even as she moves forward.

(This is part of the human condition: none of us is perfect, even if we expect we should be.) Change is a process, not a one-and-done event. We must be continuously aware of our behaviors, assess them and tweak as needed. Most importantly, we must not be judgmental, because that just inflames our shame and gets us stuck. It takes time to develop new skills.

What led you to become a Money Coach, what's your backstory?

My first family was poor, and my mother spent money like it was going out of style. As my family of origin fell apart, I become very unhappy. I moved in with an Aunt and Uncle who had more money but had unhealthy spending habits. I had a very conflicted experience and ideas about money—from "there isn't enough" to "spending money in weird ways." I felt sad and lonely and that I deserved more.

After college and entering the financial field, I had very problematic spending behaviors and racked up a lot of credit card debt to pay for big-ticket items that fed my dissonance.

I sold my home just to pay off credit cards and was on the verge of bankruptcy. Then I was introduced to a financial advisor who helped me see I would never have a peaceful relationship with money until I faced my underlying issues.

I began the lifelong commitment to the process of healing, and it turned my life around. I made the career shift to be able to help others, and I am still thrilled about this work 25 years later. Today, I feel there is very little I need. Yes, I need a safe home, safe transportation, nutritious food, good healthcare and appropriate clothing. But I no longer have to own something to bring me peace. I find peace through spirituality, family and close friends I can be honest with.

What's the most important thing people should consider when evaluating a Money Coach?

There are many styles and flavors of financial consulting. Some work strictly with budgets and financial planning. As a money coach, I work with you on the underlying emotions fueling your money behaviors.

When evaluating any financial advisor, you have to ask whether this individual will give you a positive sense of support. Or, will this individual be judgmental of your situation, and only trigger your blame and shame cycle? It makes a huge difference to work with someone who is nonjudgmental and can support you in doing the work that will bring about your lifelong change for the better.

What are your final thoughts for individuals and couples who are thinking about all aspects of their financial lives?

Patience is the most important ingredient. You must be patient with yourself, and not so hard and judgmental. You have to be the nurturing parent to yourself you've always wished for. For couples, you must be patient with each other, because you come from very different places about money.

If someone feels they want to replace shame and fear with mastery, so they can change their relationship with money, and make their own powerful money decisions, how can they connect with you?

You have to be in enough pain and feel enough suffering around your finances that you are willing to do the work. That starts with picking up the phone and calling me, from anywhere in the country. We talk about your situation and explore how I can support you. Then we can begin the work together. If you are willing to show up, continuously do the work, all the while accepting your imperfection and keep to the process, you will become a master of understanding your finances.

Spreadsheets will reveal a lot about your emotional patterns. Once you have opened up to me about the emotions behind your old money habits and set your own criteria for healthy money decisions, I can keep you mindful of line items that may not be aligned with that new criteria. I teach you a protocol and cash flow management system they you can move forward with and work independently.

If you are willing to follow this process, keep asking the questions and look at the numbers in this context, you will be successful. When you are successful, you feel a sense of mastery over the numbers and your life.

When you get clear and clean about your money, you get clear and clean about many other aspects of your life. Self-mastery over your money brings a sense of self-mastery in your life.

Visit www.KathrynAmenta.com for more information and contact. Call (415) 333-6972 to schedule an appointment.

JORDAN M. FLOWERS

Financial Advisor
Wealth Financial Services & Tax Advisory

Email: jflowers@wfsta.com
Website: www.wfsta.com/jordanflowerss
LinkedIn: www.linkedin.com/in/jordanmflowers
Twitter: www.twitter.com/jordanmsflowers
Facebook: www.facebook.com/Wfsta
Call: (847) 499-3454
Direct: (847) 499-3336

Jordan Flowers has been giving his clients peace of mind in their finances for over 12 years. He firmly believes people don't plan to fail; they fail to plan.

Since a young age, Jordan was introduced to the financial service industry, his father was a financial advisor, and he got to hear stories of financial success and stories of Financial failure from clients not having a plan. Jordan strongly believes people should have a written living plan for their finances and a goal in mind.

Jordan's clients have a written plan incorporating investments, life insurance, estate planning, Taxes, long-term care and expenses to live the lifestyle they desire. Although Jordan believes having a plan for all aspects of their finances are important he feels the most important thing the client should know is this. The client doesn't always want to know how much you know; they want to know how much you care.

RETIRE ON YOUR OWN TERMS
By Jordan Flowers

Tell us about Wealth Financial Services & Tax Advisory, the people you work with and the types of situations they find themselves in when they come to you for your help?

I help 55-70-year-old families to have a custom retirement income plan, so they can live their retirement to the fullest, without ever worrying about running out of money.

Wealth Financial Services & Tax Advisory and I strongly believe that you must put the client's interests first (sometimes this means telling them they are in a great place and they should thank their current advisor).

This should be common practice in the industry, but sadly I've seen many prospects who were put into investment vehicles that benefited the advisor and not so much the client.

We are Fiduciaries so by law we have to put the client's interest first, but I personally want to do the very best for my clients, so I can work with their kids and possibly grandchildren establishing a legacy for their family. Ensuring the clients best interest is first and foremost gives me peace of mind knowing I did everything in my power to impact their lives positively. I have been very blessed with the referrals generated by a 99% retention rate from our current clients.

Most the people that come into my office have worked hard their entire life, put their kids thru college and put away money in their 401ks they have been so busy with life they haven't fully planned for retirement that's where I can help. I work with families that don't want to worry about the next big crash in the market, families that want to focus on their family not just their finances.

Many times I have clients that are near or about to retire, and they have no idea how in retirement they are going to get the Income they need to live on, and more importantly where and when to start taking income from their 401ks, social security, pensions, other investments. These decisions are vital to the success of their retirement.

Sometimes I have families that come to me that are already in retirement, and they are looking for ways to improve their situation, or they are unhappy with their current advisor. I show these clients what Financial path they are on currently and if I can give some ideas to enhance their overall portfolio.

Since our office is full service and we prepare tax returns as well, I have people that come to us initially to have their taxes prepared for the year. Then after hearing simple techniques, I recommend to reduce their tax liability and reduce the fees they are paying they become financial clients as well.

What are the advantages of having a custom retirement income plan for 55-70-year-old families?

As I stated earlier people don't plan to fail, they fail to plan. To achieve the highest level of accomplishment in life, you need to have goals. Many people's goal is to have peace of mind and never worry about money in retirement. But few of these people have a plan to accomplish this, and they end up always thinking about money, or they get nervous when the market has a downturn. Having a simple easy to understand plan in retirement eliminates the stress and worries of the market.

Having a well-designed Retirement Income plan gives you confidence! A well-developed plan will position your money into three buckets. The money you need now, the money you need 5 or so years from now, and money you need ten years down the road. By having this structure your never forced to lock in a loss because the market has had a significant downturn.

The money you need now in your first bucket should not have any risk involved. The money you need over the next five years bucket should have little or no risk involved as well. With the last bucket being for the long term allowing it to take more risk in the market.

I see a lot of people that have a bulk or all of their retirement funds at high risk in the market and when the market has a downturn, and those clients are forced to withdraw funds, locking in a loss. Withdrawing out of your investments when the market is down could cripple and collapse your retirement.

Budget…

This word causes some individuals to cringe, but when it comes to a Retirement Income Plan, it can empower you to spend more.

How is that so?

Well having a plan can show you that you no longer have to worry about running out of money, you have minimized or eliminated the market risk in your portfolio, and you have more than enough income now to live the lifestyle you've always wanted.

Yes without fear or regret of spending money on that vacation of your dreams, or maybe it's that car you've always dreamed about? Or possibly you're taking the entire family on a vacation that you treat them too. For some of my clients, they want to benefit a charity and see first-hand how their generous spirit has benefited the lives of the charity they support.

How does having a Retirement Income Plan help me on my taxes? Taxes are the biggest expense most will pay throughout their retirement, yet few people take the needed steps to reduce or eliminate their tax liability. Many CPAs and accountants are great history teachers they explain what you receive back or what you owe from the Previous year.

When you work with a financial firm that looks at the entire picture you look forward to your Tax planning. Looking forward can help you decide what tax-friendly investments to choose, which could include using ROTH IRAs and other tax-free investment strategies. As well as possibly paying more in taxes now to reduce future tax liability. Using these simple strategies you can reduce or eliminate your tax liability.

Legacy - if you have a strong desire to leave as much as you can to your heirs a little bit of planning can create millions of benefits for your family. You may have more than enough income to support your lifestyle comfortably, but you want to give as much as possible to your kids.

Using effective planning strategies you could leave millions to your heir's tax-free and create a legacy for your family. Our firm strongly encourages all our clients to set up trusts to not only protect their assets but to have their legal documents in place to avoid causing stress to the family in the event of an emergency.

Yes, having a plan will give you confidence, empower you, and help you to reduce your taxes and possibly create a legacy for your Family that will last for generations to come.

What do you feel are the biggest myths out there when it comes to retirement planning?

Many feel like Retirement planning is so complicated and hard to understand, which is a huge myth. Retirement Planning should be clear and concise; you tell me your goals, and I create a simple plan to help you achieve them. Our financial plans are one large sheet of paper that's it.

On that sheet, we show our clients where all their income is coming from (salary, social security, pensions, etc.), as well as all of their assets and how all their assets work together to accomplish their goals. It's that simple, one piece of paper.

I love the feeling when people's eyes light up, and they understand how they are going to accomplish their goals, and for the first time in their life's they see how their investments and other sources of income all work in unison to achieve the best possible outcome.

Another myth when it comes to Retirement planning is that you need to take on a lot of risks to get competitive returns. I find this to be false with today's investment world you have so many low risk or no risk alternatives that you can develop a well-diversified strategy not taking on a lot risk.

I usually ask people if you made 30% on your investments this year would this change your lifestyle? 95% of the time the answer is no they tell me, "I probably would still spend the same amount I do anyways." Then I ask them if you were to lose 30% of your assets this year would that affect your Lifestyle? 80% of people say, "Yes that would affect their spending habits and probably affect them emotionally."

I am a sports fan, and I try to relate this to the game of football. If you have a big lead at halftime, what is even more important in the second half? Taking more risks and going on the offensive? Or controlling the game and being more defensive?

Most of the clients I work with are in the second half of the game and preparing for or in retirement. This thought process sometimes is tough to adapt to most people's lives since they've been told to be put money away in their 401k and other investments and be aggressive. Nearing or in

Retirement, the game changes and people need to change along with the game. It's no longer about how much can I make; it's how do I preserve and distribute my wealth effectively to myself and possibly the next generation.

What are some common misconceptions about the Financial Services industry?

Too many people feel like the financial services industry or financial advisors in general only focus on investments. Yes investments are a vital part of what we do, but if you work with someone as a Wealth manager, that is a holistic financial advisor that works as your ally on all phases of your Financial Life, then you will be getting much more than someone just looking at your investments.

I believe we are experiencing a major shift in the industry and that people are moving more and more to an advisor that has a team that can accomplish everything for them financially under one roof. This includes investments, tax preparation, tax planning, estate planning, Life Insurance and can give them the high level of customer service in all these areas and be there for the client for all their needs.

I also think that most people think all financial advisors offer roughly the same type of investment options. Clients need to know the type of advisor they are going too to ensure they are a good fit for their needs.

Broker Dealers are big brand name money managers that you usually see commercials for them on TV they make money on transactions usually buying and selling of securities, or they put you into certain funds that they say are a great investment, but you discover later they made more money by recommending you to invest in that fund. Broker Dealers can be a good fit for some clients, and they sometimes have well put together investment options.

Then there are banks, many people today see the brick and mortar of a bank and have a sense of security there. In 1999 the Glass–Steagall legislation went into effect allowing banks to give investment advice. This led to the 2008 crisis when banks got greedy and made these products for profit then when everything collapsed the banks got bailed out, but the average American lost a lot of money!

Many times when you go to a bank, and the teller sees you have a large sum of cash they tell you; you should talk to the investment advisor there. They maybe make some recommendations, and you possibly invest, many times the investment advisor isn't at the bank two months or 2 years later and the relationship is hard to establish.

Additionally, banks have a limited toolbox of the investments they can recommend, and I see more frequently than I'd like, banks putting clients into their own funds to make more money. Still, many people like the feeling of working with a bank and sometimes the bank have maintained a good relationship with them throughout the years.

Lastly, there is the independent Financial Advisor. These individuals have a much larger toolbox and can virtually make recommendations on most investments out there today. Think of it this way if you walked into Northwestern Mutual would they ever tell you to go to Prudential since they have a better product or investment? Obviously not, they try to promote and sell the products of their office.

Since independent advisors don't have a brand name or a large brick and mortar chain behind them, they make up for it with strong relationships and showing the clients the best company and investment options for them. They are also Fiduciaries, so they have to put the client's interest first by law.

When working with an independent Financial Advisor that has a large team that can prepare your taxes, offer you life insurance, estate planning, you can accomplish many tasks under one roof.

What are some of your client's most common fears about retirement planning?

I think the fear of the unknown is a big factor. What if I am not in a position to retire, or maybe procrastination is the problem, or they feel like it is too late to do anything at this point.

Information is power, and they need to gather the information they need to give them the power to make the right decisions. When you're afraid of knowing where you stand, you're just hurting your family. If you love your family, you'll overcome this fear and find out exactly where you stand. Maybe you're in a much better position then you thought, or maybe you have to make some adjustments.

Procrastination is a human emotion, and I believe we all experience this from time to time. Retirement can be overwhelming, and while you're still working, you might feel like you don't have time to plan for retirement.

I am sure you have taken a vacation or had a wedding or maybe made an amazing dinner. You needed a plan your vacation to ensure you got transportation, lodging and an agenda of activities. You made arrangements for the wedding, making sure you had the suits and wedding dress for that important day.

If you prepared an amazing dinner, you had a vision of what the outcome would be, and you gathered all the ingredients needed to make the meal a success. In life, your vacation may last a week, your wedding day lasts a day, and that meal lasts an hour. Yet you took the time to plan. Your retirement is the longest vacation you've ever been on, so don't procrastinate on the plan, make the vision of your dream retirement a reality.

It's too late!!!

It's never too late to plan or enhance what you're currently doing. If you're paying taxes, it means two things

1. You're making money, so that's a good thing and

2. You still can plan to lower your tax liability for you or the next generation by doing backdoor ROTH Ira conversions and other tax efficient strategies.

What if your parents didn't have a plan for long-term care and you see the costs of the nursing home eating away at all their assets, even then there are steps we can take to protect a portion of the assets. What if you don't want to leave anything to the next generation we'll we can plan on bouncing the check to the undertaker too. :)

What other perceived obstacles prevent people from seeking the help of a Financial Advisor?

Trust, who do you trust? I feel like the media and some well-known (not in a good way), Financial advisors have given our profession a bad name in some respects. Trust is something that takes a lot of time to develop but can be lost in one second. I think people need to ask questions interview advisors and see who they can trust.

How much is it going to cost?

I love answering this question actually because I think everyone should know how we can be compensated and what we do to earn that compensation. Let's be clear here, no matter where you go for investments someone is making money on your money. If you get a CD, let's say at 2%, the bank pays you two percent, but they are loaning out that money at a higher rate and making money on your money. When I ask prospects, do you know how much you're paying in fees 90% of them have no idea? Or they think they are paying one fee only to discover they are paying a lot more in fees. Every person interviewing a financial advisor should ask them how they get compensated.

Although all my 1st appointment discovery meetings are free of charge, I make it a point to address if we decided to do business together what the fees would be and what you'd be getting for those fees.

When it comes to retirement what are some of the common mistakes you see people make?

Since our firm has a Tax practice as well, I see many times a year that a prospect made a bad investment move such as triggering too much in capital gains, withdrawing too much or too little out of their IRAs and not watching how these investment decisions created thousands of dollars of unneeded tax liability. People don't sometimes realize the way our tax system is set up. One bad investment decision can create a large domino effect when it comes to Taxes.

Life Insurance reviews, many people have old policies that had a goal/purpose 10-20-30 years ago, but now they are in a different phase of their life and maybe instead of using the Life Insurance as a death benefit they want to move the Life insurance policy into another policy specifically designed for long-term care protection. I've also seen many old policies with cash value that can move their policies over to new policies and increase their death benefit times 4! This is due to life expectancy increasing giving the clients an advantage if they move over policies.

I find some families that are ultra conservative that keep a large sum of their assets in checking, savings, or CD accounts. Most of the time these accounts are not keeping up with inflation.

Whatever gains are made they are taxed on line 8A of their tax return. You should know that there are a number of safe investment alternatives that can keep you up with inflation and not incur tax liability every year.

Many people don't realize the amount of risk they are taking inside their portfolios; this is a major mistake right before or in retirement because if there is a major market correction, these clients may not see the recovery of these funds in their lifetime.

Beneficiaries - do you remember 10, 20, or 30 years ago when you first opened up some of your accounts and who you put on as the beneficiary. By having beneficiary reviews with your advisor, you won't be shocked at how many old accounts have beneficiaries that are no longer your intended beneficiary or no longer alive.

Share an example of how you have helped someone to overcome obstacles and give them peace of mind in retirement.

I had a prospect that attended one of my educational classes on Taxes in retirement; they were very upfront with me saying they liked their current advisor and had been with him for over 30 years but wanted to learn more on some tax strategies and if I could maybe help a portion of their portfolio. As with all clients, I say, "I'll create a plan for you, and if you like it, we can keep talking and move forward in doing business together, However, if you don't like the plan we can still be friends, but it won't cost you anything to see my proposal of the plan."

After getting to learn more about the client and goals they had, I continued putting the plan in place and discovered that from the amount of money they spend, if they continued the pattern, they could run out of money in 10-15 years. In addition to that, if the market were to have a correction, they could run out of money in half that time. So I explained to them some tax-saving strategies as well as my recommendations to minimize the risk in the market. Then I had to do something that I think most advisors hesitate to tell their clients.

I told them you're going to have to cut back a bit on some expenses to ensure you're going to never run out of money in the future. They told me for over 30 years they never had a plan in writing and they thanked me for my honesty and mentioned every time they asked their financial advisor for money he just sent it to them and never gave them a warning that they were on a path to run out of money in future.

They decided to move all their assets to me and as we continued to refine their retirement plan. We discovered two old life insurance policies that they were still paying into and that had cash value. With the death benefit combined being around 500k, due to longer life expectancies we were able to have the client eliminate paying any more premiums and increased the death benefit to over 1.2 million, as well as give them a long-term care benefit in case it was needed in the future.

Another example was a family that was referred to us by a current client. This family was in their mid-50's and very worried about the market and if and when they could retire and stay retired. After learning about them, I discovered since they had kids at an early age they didn't get the chance to travel and would love to travel the world when they retire.

With some planning not only did we give them peace of mind and a target date to retire for them. We put into the plan a travel fund that they have to use every year for traveling since it's part of the plan they told me not only do they enjoying traveling as a couple they have the peace of mind knowing their retirement is secure.

What inspired you to become a Financial Advisor?

At the age of 16 my parents gave me a car, well I shouldn't say gave me, they loaned me a car and had me pay 8% interest on that loan, and at the time I couldn't believe they were charging me Interest on this old Lincoln town car. Looking back, I realized that experience taught me the value of money and how you have to be wise with your money. So I paid that car off as fast as I could and began to save my money and invest it.

My father being a financial advisor taught me always to put the client first. During the summer months while in school I would help him at the office. I learned many various types of investments and strategies throughout the years. But there was one thing that I think was the turning point in my career.

I was attending one of the funerals for a client of my fathers, and my dad turned to me and told me something I'll never forget. "Son remember people don't always want to know how much you know, they want to know how much you care" I saw the clients he helped the joy and sense of accomplishment he had from helping people because he truly cared for their well-being.

I knew that I might not know everything, but I care about people, and I would care for my clients and take care of them to the best of my abilities.

Over the years my knowledge of this industry and financial topics has continued to grow. One thing has always stayed constant, the care I have for my clients, and by always putting their best interests first it gives me a peace of mind and a passion for the profession I am a part of.

What's the most important thing people approaching retirement should consider when choosing a Financial Advisor?

Work with someone that specializes in retirement planning I cannot stress this enough. Did you know most people die climbing down Mount Everest compared to climbing up? The day you Retire you are at the top of Your Financial MT Everest, Work with someone that specializes on that journey down.

Look at the other services they have to offer such as tax preparation, tax planning, estate planning, Life Insurance. Make sure you trust the individual and can have open frank conversations with them.

What are your final thoughts for 55-70-year-old families who want to live their retirement to the fullest, without ever worrying about running out of money?

If you are 55-70 years of age and preparing or maybe already in retirement, make sure you have a written plan, and a roadmap to guide you to your goals. As with anything in life, life doesn't always go to plan but when you put a plan on paper your ten times more likely to achieve your goals. When you can have all your income sources and investments work in tandem while minimizing taxes your finances will run like a fine-tuned machine propelling you to accomplish your goals.

If someone feels they want to have a custom retirement income plan, so they can live their retirement to the fullest, without ever worrying about running out of money, how can they connect with you?

Helping people is my passion, and I would love to create a Custom Retirement Income Plan for them. The first step is calling our main number **(847) 499-3454** and asking them to set up a financial appointment with Jordan.

In the first meeting, we will get a chance to know each other better and see if we are a good fit to do business in the future. I don't work with everyone, but if we feel like it's a good fit I will gather the information I need to build you a custom Retirement Income Plan.

GARY LEWIS McPHERSON II

Sr. Managing Partner
McPherson Financial Partners, LLC

Email: gary@mcphersonfp.com
Website: http://www.mcphersonfp.com
LinkedIn: www.linkedin.com/in/garymcphersonii
Call: (866) 446-3778, ext. 101
Fax: (866) 427-2260

Gary Lewis McPherson, II AIF® CLTC® has been in the financial services industry for over 16 years. Gary's financial services career began at an alternative investment group as the Assistant Fund Administrator managing the administration department for 10 public and private managed futures funds.

Gary became FINRA registered in 2008 and continued his career by partnering with a veteran financial advisor of a large insurance organization. He focused on financial planning, investments, and retirement income planning for individual clients at various net worth and income levels.

Gary founded his own practice in 2013, with Broker/Dealer Cambridge Investment Research. As the Sr. Managing Partner of McPherson Financial Partners, LLC (MFP), and specializes in comprehensive financial planning, investment management, and retirement income planning.

Gary is an independent financial advisor. He works with business owners, individuals, and professional athletes. He creates strategies to overcome the financial challenges to reach clients goals.

IT'S NOT YOUR PARENT'S RETIREMENT
By Gary Lewis McPherson II

Tell us about McPherson Financial Partners, the clients you work with and the types of situations they find themselves in when they come to you for your help?

We help pre-retirees prepare assets and build plans for retirement, so they can feel confident in their retirement goals.

Preparing your assets starts with the evaluation of your risk tolerance to know the appropriate amount of risk for your investments. Then, we work with you to evaluate your current expenses to create a list of your potential retirement expenses.

These evaluations along with your retirement time horizon are the foundation of your retirement planning which allows us to create strategies to match your customized retirement goals and plan.

Most individuals we initially meet are unsure of their retirement goals and if they are on-track. Some of this uncertainty is due to the fact that, this is not your parent's retirement.

With global financial markets, unprecedented social and technological changes of today, the average investor needs support to prepare for the future.

There are more challenges facing today's retirees than ever before.

Some of those challenges are:

- The retirement age of Social Security rising,

- More retirees are working after their formal retirement

- People living longer

- Rising healthcare costs.

These are examples of some of the reasons that pre-retirees need a plan for retirement. Preparing your assets appropriately and creating a retirement plan to match goals is the main way to limit the impact of these issues.

What are the advantages of preparing assets and building cash flow plans for retirement?

There many advantages to preparing your assets and creating a retirement plan. It starts with identifying your retirement goal and knowing where you are in your retirement savings process. Everything we do is a process to ensure that we don't miss anything, or we know how to adapt to changes in your life. If you were planning for retirement as a single person, but then you get married, your retirement goal has greatly changed, but it may not change the actions in your plan. Without a plan, you would be back at the beginning, not knowing your goal and if you are on track.

When we prepare your assets, we take the global financial markets into consideration along with your risk tolerance and time horizon. This limits us reacting to the constantly changing volatile markets because we have planned for the volatility.

With few pensions remaining, individuals need to create their own income plans. These income plans are customized to your retirement goals, and they can face challenges like age gaps between married couples when a spouse is more than five years younger than the other spouse.

Lastly, the retirement plan needs to be tested and incorporate all healthcare costs, like co-pays and medicine, which many individuals don't account for in retirement planning or when using a retirement calculator.

What do you feel are some of the biggest myths about retirement planning?

There are many myths towards retirement planning. It starts with the believing that rules of thumb work for everyone. That is why individuals need a customized plan to match their unique needs.

There is the myth that investing in your corporate retirement plan and Social Security will be enough for your retirement needs. Without an evaluation of your current and future expenses, we don't know if that will be enough to meet retirement income needs.

An expensive myth is delaying your retirement savings until the last 10 - 20 years of employment. The truth is that the earlier that you save, the more prepared you will be for your retirement goals. Even if you won't receive a corporate match, your retirement savings is crucial in your preparation. Also, your debt reduction goals are not typically more important than retirement savings. They are equally important goals, and one shouldn't supersede the other. You need to have goals aligned to create your financial security.

A common myth is that the Social Security system will fail or not provide for individuals in the future. It is not realistic to expect the complete failure of Social Security in today's political environment. It is more realistic that the payouts will be reduced in the future. This is another reason that you need a plan that can adapt to current changes. This is just as common as the myth that Medicare is the only healthcare that you need in retirement and it is free. Part A, the hospital part, of Medicare, is at no-cost, but there is a cost for Part B, the health insurance part of Medicare. Most retirees need supplemental insurance to cover pharmacy costs and co-insurance costs during retirement.

Another retirement income myth I sometimes come across is that your expenses will greatly reduce during retirement, which is not always true. Many people utilize 90-100% of their pre-retirement income during retirement, which is why we start with an evaluation of your expenses. This is just as common as thinking that your income will reduce, and you will not have any taxes. This can vary greatly depending on your state of residence. Also, the amount of income, whether from pension or investments can influence whether your Social Security income is taxable.

A common myth about investing while in retirement is that you will have 100% of your assets in relatively safe investments like CDs and Bonds. The problem that this myth ignores is inflation and purchasing power. You need your assets to grow to keep up with inflation and last as long as you need them.

The last myth that we will review is long-term care. This is not just an evaluation of insurance that covers nursing home expenses; it includes funds to cover costs to alter your home for your medical needs, getting assistance to remain in your home, and for other assisted living expenses. This is something that should be planned for early to ensure that you are prepared. If you need or decide to purchase long-term care insurance, you need to qualify for it and have the funds to purchase it. As we get older, it gets more difficult to qualify for this type of insurance and more expensive to purchase. We help you evaluate your risk and plan for this risk.

What are some common misconceptions about the Finance industry?

A common misconception about the Finance industry is that all financial advisors; whether advisors, planners, and/or representatives are the same. There is a large difference in the education, experience, and knowledge of financial advisors. Also, there is a large difference with the affiliation of the financial advisor; whether they are a captive advisor/agent/ representative, an independent advisor, or a Registered Investment Advisor (RIA). Some of these affiliations have inherent conflicts of interest. You should ask for an advisor's ADV and their bio to evaluate their capabilities. Also, you should ask them what type of representative they are and how they are different from the others. I have worked for, and with many of the types, so I know the differences well.

Another misconception is that a large firm or bank more well-known can do a better job. That has nothing to do with the advisor's ability to assist individuals. You need to focus on your advisor and his/her capabilities to assist you. The company or broker-dealer that the advisor works with has no bearing on how your accounts should be managed. Some firms are less known because they have smaller advertising budgets than larger firms or banks.

What are some of the most common fears about retirement planning?

Common fears about retirement planning are that they will never be able to retire. Another common fear is that they will have to work until age 70 or later. This is why it is important to start early.

Another common fear is that their money will not last long enough. We need to evaluate your expenses to know your true retirement income goal and evaluate your needs. We need to stress test your assets to know the probability that they will last throughout your retirement.

Healthcare is another common fear, and it should be incorporated into your retirement planning. This will minimize the impact that it may cause.

Lastly, is the common fear of investment losses while in retirement. If your assets are properly prepared and allocated this should be minimized. There are many different ways to reduce investment risk during retirement, but it is not just investing in relatively safe investments like Cds and Bonds.

What should the people you work with do to get past those fears?

My clients are educated on risks during retirement. We create a retirement plan to minimize these risks. The plan is their roadmap to retire and solve their questions about when retirement can begin and how it should progress. This increases their clarity and confidence in achieving their retirement goals. The planning allows us to be proactive and not reactive.

What other perceived obstacles might be preventing people from seeking help?

Some perceived obstacles that prevent people from seeking help costs, fear, and over-confidence.

The costs of working with an advisor should be reasonable and based on the services that an individual receives. You should find an advisor that can offer a complimentary initial evaluation. Then they should provide you the information of the costs for the services that you need.

Individuals have fears that they may not have enough assets to work with an advisor. Meet with an advisor and let them give you an evaluation of what you have and what you need. They should then be able to tell you if it makes sense for you to work with an advisor. As a fiduciary, I am obligated to work in a client's best interest, and it starts with the initial evaluation.

Another fear is that you are not prepared for retirement. It is better to know and start your planning now, than waiting until it is too late, and it causes you to make significant sacrifices in retirement.

Overconfidence is the fact that you don't need an Advisor. You are able to evaluate your investment yourself, and the retirement calculator says that you are on-target. Many studies have shown that individual investors do not outperform managed accounts.

Also, the retirement calculator is based on the information that you input. If there are expenses that you don't account for or miss, then they will not be in the output. It is always better to have a second opinion to ensure that you don't forget or miss something.

When it comes to retirement planning, what are some of the common pitfalls and mistakes you see people make?

One of the key mistakes that people make with retirement planning is starting late.

Another common mistake is to invest without evaluating your risk tolerance and your retirement goals.

Cash management is a key to retirement planning and developing your goals.

How can these pitfalls or mistakes be avoided?

You should start as soon as possible. Also, you should do more than just your employer retirement plan. Some people can also contribute to a Roth IRA even after contributing to your employer retirement plan.

You should always evaluate your risk tolerance and match it with your retirement goals to create your portfolio. This reduces reactive actions that could hurt your portfolio.

Cash management is helpful now, but it is critical when you are no longer working. When you are retired, you typically have a fixed income, and you need to manage your expenses within that income.

Share an example of how you have helped individuals to overcome these obstacles and succeed in feeling confident in their retirement goals.

Through my years of experience, I have seen many different retirement planning scenarios. It is common for individuals not to know what their retirement goals are and whether they are prepared. You can't be confident if you don't know your preparedness.

Another common situation is for individuals to create their portfolios based on their fears. This typically leads to them investing in non-aggressive investments like stable value funds or investing in insurance products.

These types of investments might not be suitable for the individuals to meet their retirement goals. We utilize our system of starting with your risk tolerance evaluation, then evaluating your goals/needs, and creating a retirement plan to achieve your goals/needs based on this information. We replace any products that don't meet the goals of your plan, if possible or work around those products to accomplish your goals.

What inspired you to become a Financial Advisor, what's your backstory?

I have a degree in Psychology with a focus on Organizational Psychology. Organizational Psychology comprehensively evaluates workers to find opportunities or positions that optimize their abilities to increase the productivity of the organization. I later obtained my Business Management degree with a minor in financial planning. Financial planning is like Organization Psychology, where it is a comprehensive evaluation of an individual's current assets/state and creates a plan to optimize their assets to reach their goals. I quickly realized that everyone needs this type of assistance, whether they are aware of it or not. It can make such a positive impact on their confidence and their possible success.

I wish that someone that could have helped my parents prepare and they would be in much better retirement situations than they are now. Even an initial evaluation to guide them in the right direction could have had a great effect. A key example is long-term care insurance, which my parents can't qualify for and can't afford at this point. This restricts their future retirement as their medical needs increase.

What's the most important thing people should consider when evaluating a Financial Advisor?

The first thing that people should consider when evaluating an advisor is whether they have the education, experience, and knowledge to help you. You should then know if your advisor is working as a fiduciary for you. This should ensure that they are working in your best interest. You should understand how the advisor is compensated and what services are included in that compensation. Lastly, you need to know if there any conflicts of interest for the advisor to work with you. Will they be recommending proprietary products, or do they get added incentives for selling a product? The product selection should be based on your retirement plan to achieve your goals.

What are your final thoughts for anyone who wants to feel confident and gain clarity in their retirement goals?

Meet with a financial advisor and have them evaluate your current situation and goals. Make sure your plan is based on your risk tolerance, your goals, and your time horizon. Again, it never hurts to get a second opinion to know that you have what you need or you are doing enough.

Start as soon as possible to ensure that you are prepared.

Price is not the only factor. You pay healthcare costs to ensure your health and your retirement planning is as important as your health to ensure your livelihood in retirement.

If someone feels they want to prepare assets and build cash flow plans for retirement, so they can feel confident in their retirement goals, how can they connect with you and what will happen when they do?

It starts with a conversation for me to understand your situation. For a free one hour consultation, please contact me at 866-446-3778, ext. 101 or via email at gary@mcphersonfp.com. We will review your current situation and then decide on the next steps. I am a phone call or email away to assist you.

DAVID EDWARDS, MBA

Wealth Advisor
President & Founder, Heron Wealth

Email: DavidEdwards@HeronWealth.com
Website: https://www.HeronWealth.com
LinkedIn: Linkedin.com/in/DavidEdwardsMBA
Facebook: https://Facebook.com/DavidEdwardsHeronWealth
Twitter: https://Twitter.com/HeronWealth
Office: 347 580-5288 | **Cell: 917 705-3893**
Fax: 347 580-5288

David Edwards is president and founder of Heron Wealth, which provides financial planning, investment advice and estate planning to individuals and families across the United States and in Europe.

David graduated from Hamilton College with a concentration in History and Mathematics and holds an MBA in General Management from Darden Graduate School of Business at the University of Virginia.

David contributed over 100 columns to TheStreet.com. David is quoted frequently in Bloomberg, Wall Street Journal, Reuters, InvestmentNews, Money, Financial Planning and many other financial news sources. David Edwards is a member of the Investment Adviser Association serving on the Government Relations and Technology committees and is an advisory board member for eMoney. Prior to founding Heron Wealth, Edwards was associated with Morgan Stanley, JP Morgan and Nomura Securities developing investment products and quantitative trading models.

David competes in sailing regattas from New England to the Caribbean and coaches a hometown team in New York Harbor.

THE GLIDEPATH TO RETIREMENT
By David Edwards

Tell us about Heron Wealth, the clients you work with and the types of situations they find themselves in when they come to you for your help?

Why do we talk about, "The Glidepath to Retirement?"

When a jetliner flies from London to New York, the aircraft does not arrive at JFK at 35,000 feet, then suddenly drop to the runway.

An hour in advance of arrival, while the plane is still cruising above the North Atlantic, the pilot reviews a checklist which includes: calling ahead to air control to find out about local weather; alerting the cabin crew to prepare for landing; placing the aircraft in gradual descent on the approach to Long Island; calculating the heading to the runway; extending the flaps for flight at low speed; and, most importantly, lowering and locking the landing gear.

We know the pilots that don't use checklists because annually in the United States 100 aircraft land with the landing gear is the "up" position, which is both dangerous and expensive!

Plenty of financial planning literature calls for families to start planning for retirement in their 20's, and we know that's not realistic. People in their 20, 30's and 40's are focused on getting married, starting families and businesses, buying property, paying for children's educations. We find that age 50, 55, or even 60, when a family is still 10-15 years away from retirement, is a good time to engage a "pilot" to establish and review their "retirement checklist." A family certainly could prepare for retirement without our experience, but if that family only gets one chance to "land the plane," getting their retirement plan wrong could be catastrophic.

Our clients are successful executives, business owners, and rising professionals. We seek to optimize every element of a family's financial plan to achieve short-term goals now while ensuring an enjoyable and comfortable retirement later.

How early should a family start planning for retirement?

Generally, we find that about the time a family has already addressed other major financial concerns such as buying a home and funding the children's education, the next major question is: how to fund their retirement? Of course, every family has unique and different circumstances. Some families are couples without children, who don't need to worry about education expense and, therefore, can spend money on other luxuries. Some families are single persons, who may need extra confidence in their retirement plan given that individuals are entirely dependent on their own resources. Regardless of circumstances, we can start from a client's intake questionnaire and prepare a personal balance sheet, 5-year cash flow report and lifetime WealthTrack in about two hours. From good data, comes good decisions. We can show the family what their future looks like in the present, and also show how decisions made today will affect their retirement 15 years from now. As we like to say, "We are in the business of converting fear into joy!"

What do you feel are the biggest myths when it comes to retirement planning?

The most dangerous myth is that "we can figure this out the day we retire." Without a clear understanding of retirement cash flows from Social Security, pensions and retirement accounts, offset by living, housing, and medical expenses, families can grossly underestimate their preparation for retirement.

Our firm employs the most advanced financial planning tools available. We can readily develop a "base case" scenario from the current facts. We know a client's current income, spending, retirement and investment account accounts, real estate equity and can approximate their longevity based on their parent's history. We can show a family whether their current assets will grow sufficiently by retirement to last the rest of their lives, or whether there might be a shortfall.

This information is extremely valuable 10 or 15 years in advance of retirement because we have plenty of time to explore alternatives. This information is far less valuable the day OF retirement, so don't delay in starting the conversation.

What are some common misconceptions about the Finance industry?

The most prevalent misconception about the financial services industry is that registered investment advisers, financial planners, and sales representatives are all the same. In fact, advisers adhere to different business models, are compensated differently and are regulated differently.

We believe that the general public should only seek advice from advisers such as Heron Wealth who operate under the "fiduciary standard" as defined in the Investment Advisers Act of 1940 and are regulated directly by the Securities and Exchange Commission (SEC.) The fiduciary standard is pretty specific in defining that the advisor must ALWAYS place the client's interests ahead of his or her own, must be fully transparent about ALL costs and fees associated with an investment, must diligently choose the BEST possible investments for a client, and must avoid conflicts of interest. Generally, advisers operating under the fiduciary standard will invoice clients directly for fees, either as a percentage of assets under management, or as per hour financial planning fees, and receive no compensation for product sales.

There are other financial advisors, including traditional brokers at banks and brokerages and sales representatives at insurance companies, who operate under the "suitability standard." Their advice does NOT have to be the best possible advice, merely the minimally suitable advice. These advisers are often paid through embedded and undisclosed commissions, which enables the advisers to position their advice as "free." Brokers and variable annuity sales reps are regulated by Financial Industry Regulatory Authority

(FINRA,) an industry trade association, not the SEC, an agency of the US federal government.

What are your clients' most common fears about planning for retirement?

The human brain is designed for a far simpler era of finding food, finding a mate and avoiding tigers. Retirement is NOTHING as scary as a saber tooth tiger, yet many families envision worst-case scenarios of running out of money and ending up homeless - even with millions in their investment accounts.

Instead of retirement, we talk to our clients about "rewirement" - what would you do if working for a living was optional? Travel is probably the number 1 interest, as is the pursuit of experiences in general (things like houses, cars, jewelry become less interesting over time.) The ability to contribute one's experience in a pro-bono setting comes up often. The ability to support the next generation, for example, by contributing to a grandchild's education, is also often a priority.

When we reframe retirement as a process to be played out over a decade or two instead of an all or nothing event hard-coded to a specific age, we can take the time to make good decisions. We have a client who worked like a crazy person right out of college and had the good fortune to able to retire at age 40. After a couple of years of playing golf, he was so bored that he "unretired." This time around, instead of being an entrepreneur, he positioned himself as a consultant to entrepreneurs, which enabled him to satisfy his natural creativity but strike a better balance between work and life (he and his wife travel for 12 weeks of the year, for example.)

There are some specific fears that can be addressed with planning.

1. The fear of running out of money. While nothing in investing is guaranteed, financial planners have decades of experience determining sustainable draw rates in retirement. The available studies show that a properly diversified portfolio (balanced between stocks, bonds and cash, and including some international exposure) can distribute 4% conservatively, 5%/year aggressively and never run out of money. Among our own client base, even during the financial crisis of 2008-9, we never had to cut a client's draw rate who maintained distribution rates in these ranges.

    If a family has $1 million on retirement day, they can draw $40K conservatively, $50K aggressively per year. Naturally the more money a family has, the more a family can draw. As long as a family remains pragmatic about their spending (either spend less in retirement or save more while working) they will never run out of money.

2. Social Security won't be there when I need it. Unfortunately, half of American families have no retirement savings at all. Though pundits worry that Social

Security will "run out of money in 2034," the bottom line is that politicians aren't going to allow grandparents to starve in the streets - Social Security will be there in some form or another. There are quite a few things that can be done to fix the funding gap - raise the age of full retirement, increase or eliminate the salary cap for FICA deductions, cut the "cost-of-living" adjustment. For many of the families we work with, Social Security will provide the first $35-60K of a family's income in retirement.

3. Health care costs in retirement could wipe out a family's savings. This is not an unreasonable concern as unplanned medical expenses are the # 1 reason why average families end up in bankruptcy and foreclosure. Families should consider purchasing Long Term Care Insurance policies by their early-mid 50s. With each passing year, the policies become ever more expensive and may become unaffordable when a family reaches their mid-60's.

Medicare is actually pretty good insurance - "The best we've ever had" according to one of our client families. But also investigate Medigap insurance plans as well, particularly as Medicare does not provide coverage if you travel outside the US.

What should successful executives, business owners, and rising professionals do to get past those fears?

Start the conversation! Before we work with you, we must know you. No architect would bring building blueprints to the first meeting with a client, and neither do we. We have no preconceptions about how we will advise you until we have completed a process of mutual discovery. We have broken up our onboarding process into six easy steps.

1: Hot Topic

Individuals and families reach out to us most often after a transitional life event: a new job or a big promotion, getting married, starting a family, inheriting money, selling a business or getting divorced. An essential part of our initial information gathering is identifying what keeps you up at night.

2: Base-Plan

We ask you to provide us with the information we need to create your financial base-plan. This plan will include an analysis of your income sources, living expenses, major projected expenses such as college tuition, assets such as investments and real estate and liabilities such as a mortgage and credit cards.

3: First Review

In this meeting, over the phone or in person, we will show you the base-plan, fill in gaps in our knowledge of your situation and answer any questions you may have.

4: Advisory Agreement

The provision of financial advice creates rights and responsibilities for both the client and advisor. After our first planning meeting, we'll ask you to review and sign our agreement. You can cancel this agreement at any time.

5: Details

In subsequent meetings and phone calls, we finalize the details of your financial plan together with you. We explain how we address your various financial needs.

6: Onboarding

If you have asked us to manage your investment accounts, we align your accounts with a single custodian. We adjust your asset allocation to match your investment plan and divide your assets between taxable and tax-deferred account in minimizing your current tax bill. We train you on how you can make the most of using your personal client dashboard so that you can access many financial planning tools and reports from your phone, tablet, or personal computer at any time.

What other perceived obstacles do you see that might be preventing successful executives, business owners, and rising professionals from seeking the help of a Wealth Advisor?

Bernie Madoff and the 2008-9 financial crisis blew apart the "presumption of trust" that advisers such as ourselves enjoyed for most of the last 50 years. When the news of Madoff's arrest first flashed across our Bloomberg screen, we thought it was a joke. Within 24 hours, we realized that the story was true, and we immediately sent a bulletin to all our clients explaining what we knew about the situation and also about the safeguards we had put in place to protect our clients from such a scenario. Specifically:

1. Assets are always held by a qualified custodian, never by Heron Wealth. Each month Heron Wealth produces a client statement which MUST match up with the custodial statement, sent separately by the custodian to the client - "Trust but verify!"

2. Heron Wealth has no access to a client's cash or securities, other than to submit an invoice for the monthly advisory fee

3. All transfers in or out of a client's account take place via Electronic Funds Transfer over established signed standing instructions between a client's custodial and bank account, or over a signed wire transfer.

4. We only invest in publicly traded securities that are priced at a minimum daily (in the case of mutual funds) or continuously (Stocks, bonds, exchange-traded funds.)

5. We do not invest in hedge funds, venture capital, limited partnerships, fund of funds, private equity or any investment vehicles with limited price transparency or liquidity.

6. There is no lock-up in any investments that we make, and there is no lockup investing with our firm - you can cancel your relationship at any time.

7. We do not commingle clients' assets.

8. We cheerfully provide references!

Every advisor with these safeguards in place adheres to the "Standard of Care" that is obligatory under the Fiduciary Standard

When it comes to planning for retirement, what are some of the common pitfalls and mistakes you see successful executives, business owners, and rising professionals make?

When we onboard a new client family, two of the universal issues we address are:

1. Over-reliance on company stock

2. Not understanding the difference between volatility and risk, and therefore having an asset allocation that is too conservative in retirement accounts.

On many occasions, an executive can end up with a substantial position in a single stock through restricted stock and stock options grant. If the company is high performing, like Amazon, for example, the family can see their wealth leap skyward daily. Emotionally, it becomes very difficult to get off that roller coaster, mainly because every sale triggers a tax bill.

Sadly, we have plenty of examples of families whose entire wealth was tied to a single stock and who lost everything. Enron's stock price quintupled between 1995 and 2000 but plunged to $0 by the end of 2001. General Electric was an original component of the Dow Jones Industrials (dating back to 1896). The stock peaked in value in 2000 but currently trades at ¼ of that peak value. For a century, GE was one of the most admired companies in the world - only a fool would sell that stock. Yet, if you're an executive of GE who retired in 2000 and depended on the GE dividend for your retirement income, that dividend was cut 36% in June 2018 and may be reduced another 30% by December 2018. Ouch!

The solution is to take the emotion out of the sales decision by establishing periodic sales plans. For executive officers who have "inside knowledge" of a company's revenues and profit forecasts, we establish "10b5-1 plans," which are named after an SEC rule designed to allow for periodic stock sales without violating "insider trading" rules. For less senior employees who are not obliged to file 10b5-1 plans, we can still create informal plans such as, "each quarter we will sell 10% of unrestricted stock positions if the stock price is over X, and we will exercise 20% of vested stock option positions that are at least 200% in the money."

Much of our work centers around dividing a family's assets into buckets with different "purposes" - this bucket is for the tax bill due next quarter; this bucket is for the children's college tuition in 5 years; this bucket is for retirement assets that the family will start drawing on in 20 years. The longer the time period until a draw on the assets in the bucket, the more aggressive the investment strategy. For example, if you have a tax bill due in a few months, the only prudent investment is cash. For a need that is 1-5 years in the future, bonds and bond funds are appropriate. For five years and out, stocks and equity funds are appropriate, yet often we see 401K retirement accounts that are heavily invested in cash and bond funds and only lightly invested in equity funds.

Families often make the mistake that they should be "conservative" with their retirement assets and invest in such a way that the account does not fluctuate much in value. People presume that volatility equals risk. No! Risk is <u>the chance money won't be there when you need it.</u> When the need is well in the future, a family SHOULD invest in volatile assets, which are also the highest returning assets. As the time to retirement comes closer, we make adjustments to the family's overall asset allocation - perhaps 80/20 in their 40's, 75/25 in their 50's, 70/30 in their 60's, 65/35 when they retire for good. A "gradual descent to the runway" over 15 years? Yes!

How can these mistakes be avoided?

Why do we pay $45 to have Jiffy Lube change the oil in our car instead of just buying 5 quarts of oil for $19 and doing the job ourselves?

1. It's a messy job.

2. You have to dispose of the waste oil.

3. The cost of replacing your engine if you screw up is $4500.

Working with a professional such as an architect, a dentist and of course a pilot, saves time and money! These days, a wealth advisor provides modest value in picking investments.

Of far greater value:

- Systematically rebalancing portfolios to "Sell high and buy low."

- Finding the lowest cost investments (passive ETF's instead of actively managed mutual funds)

- Clarifying and simplifying account structures

- Spending strategies to optimize for taxes when providing retirement income

- Behavioral coaching (protecting clients from their own worst instincts)

Good advisors earn their fees!

Share an example of how you have helped successful executives, business owners, and rising professionals to overcome these obstacles and succeed in feeling confident about their future.

One of our favorite families first connected with our firm in late 2000. Stephen*, a 35-year-old mid-level executive, married with a newborn and a toddler, called and asked,

"David, I know I don't have your account minimum, but I enjoy your column in TheStreet.com, and I wondered if you would work with me?" "Of course!" I said. As we underwent the initial discovery process, we learned that Stephen wanted, of course, a secure retirement and funding for the children's education. He also had two stretch goals - a vacation home in New England and a Porsche sports car.

Over the next 18 years, Stephen and wife Daphne* diligently saved about 15% of their income in a combination of taxable, retirement and college (529) savings plans, and we prudently invested those savings. About eight years into the relationship, Stephen bought the Porsche and bought the vacation home a few years ago. The first child went to college last fall. At our recent review, I asked Stephen what else he wanted to accomplish. He said, "Well, I would like to buy a second Porsche, but if I do that, I'll need to build a larger garage." "We can do that!" I replied.

There was nothing magical about how we achieved this. Consider that from 2001 through 2018, there were two bear markets including the "Great Recession of 2008-9." There was a horrible terrorist attack on 9/11/01. The United States ended up in two major wars that we're still fighting. We have also had two decades of "culture war" between the red and blue parts of the United States. Despite all this, people show up every day to work at McDonalds, Pfizer, Apple and thousands of other corporations and try to figure out to sell more products that are better. In the long run, the only drivers of stock market value are revenues earnings and interest rates. If we never lose sight of these fundamentals, the investing takes care of itself.

As wealth advisors, we achieve success for our clients by guiding them among ten thousand choices; help clients find the ten choices that matter the most, and provide the solutions to implement those decisions.

Names changed for privacy

What inspired you to become a Wealth Advisor, what's your backstory?

I first started investing when I was 17 years old. In those days, to research a company, you would find an envelope and a stamp, write a letter to General Electric, drop the letter off at the post office and wait. Six weeks later, you would receive a copy of the company annual report, which you would read back to front knowing that the information was anywhere from 3-9 months out of date. I was entirely self-taught, and my investing style was entirely "hit or miss."

I joined Morgan Stanley in 1983, not in wealth management but in systems, using IBM mainframes to build trading models for the fixed income department. I worked 6 ½ days/week for four years during a period of exhilarating innovation in financial products - mortgage-backed securities, collateralized mortgage obligations, swaps, and derivatives. I spent an additional four years as a management consultant to JP Morgan Securities and Nomura Securities building trading models and value at risk models. I applied the modeling skills of my fixed income work to my personal portfolio of equities. In time, I realized that only 20% of a specific company's stock price movement was associated with the company's actual numbers; 30% of the return came from the stock's sector classification, while 50% came from simply being IN the stock market. Our primary research driver today remains quantitative, but we also apply qualitative and technical screens in our research.

Eventually, I came to a crossroads in my career - did I stay on the consulting side and hire more consultants to work for me, or did I use my investment skills to manage money for other people. I thought the second option was more interesting, but I realized that if I wanted to run an investment firm, I would have to spend time in business school to pick up missing skills in marketing and operations. I attended Darden Graduate School of Business, University of Virginia, wrote the business plan for a stock picking business, graduated and commenced operations with two clients.

In the early years, I concentrated on acquiring individuals as clients because I did not have a five-year institutional track record. I saw my purpose as figuring out which mid-cap growth stocks could beat the Russell 2000 by two %/year. When clients asked me questions like, "What about my retirement?" "What about my child's education?" "What about my aging parents?" "What about my divorce?" I would reply, "Ask your accountant, ask your lawyer, ask your financial planner." Eventually, I realized that my clients saw me as "the guy with his hands on my money," and they wanted those answers from me. So I educated myself about all aspects of wealth management, not only investment management but also financial planning, tax planning, and estate planning.

Even so, I still thought of myself as a stock picker until we reviewed the results of a client survey in 2006. On the top 10 list of why clients worked with us, investment performance was the 6th most important criteria. The most important criteria? Trust! One client wrote, "Good news or bad, you will always hear first from Dave." We realized we were no longer in the investment management business; we were in the "good advice" business. From that day forward, we were no longer "investment managers" but "wealth advisors."

What's the most important thing successful executives, business owners, and rising professionals should consider when evaluating a Wealth Advisor?

When you work with an accountant, you'll speak with that professional once, perhaps twice a year. When you work with a trust and estate attorney, you speak with that professional once, perhaps twice a decade.

When you work with a wealth advisor, you will connect with that advisor on every important transition in your life - when you change jobs, get stock options, get married, have a child, send that child to college, get divorced, get remarried, worry about your parents, buy property, buy more property, deal with an injury or sickness, grieve over the death of a spouse, a parent or even a child. You must LIKE, KNOW and TRUST your wealth advisor, because that person is going to live those transitions with you for years, even decades.

At Heron Wealth, I specialize in successful executives and business owners because I am a successful executive and business owner. Any life transition that my clients can anticipate, I've already experienced. The sons and daughters of my clients, rising professionals in their 20's and 30's work with another advisor in my office who herself is rising professional, who understands their career demands, roommate situations and need to text. Other advisors in our office have other specialties - "Like attracts like!"

Probably the greatest tell, "Would I be comfortable inviting my wealth advisor to a dinner party with my friends? If "Yes," you're probably on the right track.

What are your final thoughts for successful executives, business owners and rising professionals who are considering their financial future?

Treat planning for your retirement as if you were drafting a 5-year strategic plan for your business. Assemble all available facts, compile into a base case, make projections and test alternatives.

Don't be shy to admit that you need help - you plan for retirement for one time in your life; we plan for scores of clients' retirements every day. Call us!

If someone feels they want to plan for retirement, so they can feel confident about their future, how can they connect with you and what will happen when they do?

The initial two-hour consultation is complimentary, so what is the risk of starting a conversation? Visit our website - https://www.HeronWealth.com - and learn what we do. If you feel like our advice will enable you to achieve your goals, call David Edwards on 800 99-HERON or direct on 347 580-5288 to schedule an appointment.

ABOUT THE AUTHOR

Mark Imperial is a Best Selling Author, Syndicated Business Columnist, Syndicated Radio Host, and internationally recognized Stage, Screen, and Radio Host of numerous business shows spotlighting leading experts, entrepreneurs, and business celebrities.

His passion is discovering noteworthy business owners, professionals, experts, and leaders who do great work, and sharing their stories and secrets to their success with the world on his syndicated radio program titled "Remarkable Radio."

Mark is also the media marketing strategist and voice for some of the world's most famous brands. You can hear his voice over the airwaves weekly on Chicago radio and worldwide on iHeart Radio.

Mark is a Karate black belt, teaches kickboxing, loves Thai food, House Music, and his favorite TV show is infomercials.

Learn more:

www.MarkImperial.com
www.ImperialAction.com
www.RemarkableRadioShow.com